Stephen Eno, father of Henry. Courtesy of New York State Library, Albany, New York.

TWENTY YEARS ON THE

PACIFIC SLOPE

Letters of Henry Eno from California and Nevada, 1848–1871

Edited and with an Introduction
by W. Turrentine Jackson

New Haven and London: Yale University Press 1965

917.9443
En64

To SAMUEL GUY KONE and
THE MEMORY OF MARILEE FISHER KONE
who, like the Enos, experienced the
joys and vicissitudes of life with
philosophical understanding

PREFACE

THE HENRY ENO letters from California and Nevada have been described as "one of the most interesting group of letters to have appeared in some years."* Twenty years of travel took Eno to out-of-the-way places on the Pacific Slope about which there is a dearth of information. His story is not merely another account or diary of the gold-rush era; it is even more closely related to the events on the West Coast after this period of high excitement was past. Eno's initial years were spent at Mokelumne Hill, a thriving mining camp, where professional men and politicians who were later to gain great prominence and success in the state of California were among his friends and associates. Here Henry Eno, like many men who came to the West in search of gold, became a small-time entrepreneur, was victimized by forces largely beyond his control, was wiped out financially, and forced to turn to other means of making a living.

Eno's detailed observations of Alpine County, California, from 1865 to 1869 are priceless because no history of the area has ever been written, and the most reliable sources available are the scattered and broken files of county newspapers like the *Monitor Gazette, The Alpine Miner,* and *The Alpine Chronicle,* the last of which Eno edited for a time. Unfortunately not a single issue of this newspaper has

*Dale Morgan, *California Manuscripts: Being a Collection of Important, Unpublished & Unknown Original Historical Sources,* Catalogue 159 (New York, Edward Eberstadt, 1961).

been located for the early period in which he was editor; the first issue available to scholars is that of June 16, 1866, in the Bancroft Library. In this sparsely populated mountain county Eno became a minor politician, and his correspondence reveals both the techniques and the troubles of those who assumed this role. Events in Alpine County also clearly illustrate the problem of frontier governments prematurely organized and saddled with a bureaucracy that the citizenry was unable to support.

In 1868 and 1869 silver was uncovered at White Pine in eastern Nevada, precipitating a rush that was probably the shortest yet most intense one in the history of the West. Here was the new El Dorado and Henry Eno was among the thousands who hastened to the mining district. Interest in the new "Silverland" was so acute that most letters written from White Pine ended up in the hands of some local newspaper editor, who published them for the information of his subscribers. The only letters from White Pine in manuscript form that have turned up in a systematic search of the regional libraries and depositories are those written by Henry Eno.

Some of the letters also give information about a fourth region in which Eno traveled—the scattered mining districts of the Mojave Desert and Death Valley—thus providing additional source material.

Perhaps more important, the Eno documents are a chronicle of one man's life on the Pacific Coast, a self-portrait of an interesting individual, knowledgable about life, courageous and persevering. A lawyer by training, pioneer and gold seeker by inclination, Eno reveals himself as a man well educated and widely read, a keen observer of the unfolding scenes around him, philosopher and dreamer, and an eternal optimist. Not only does he report on the changing

scene in California and Nevada from 1849 to 1871, but his
career epitomizes the valiant struggle of the western pioneers, particularly those whose fate led them into mining
communities.

Henry Eno's letters, and those of his brothers, William
and Edward, were preserved by members of the family.
Eventually they came into the hands of manuscript collec-
tors, who broke up the collection into parcels that were
readily marketable and sold them to various interested libraries. The Henry Eno letters published in this volume
were eventually acquired by Edward Eberstadt & Sons of
New York City.

My indebtedness to Dale Morgan is great, for he first
directed my attention to the Eno letters in connection with
the research on my book *Treasure Hill: Portrait of a Silver
Mining Camp* (Tucson, University of Arizona Press, 1963).
The manuscripts published herein can now be examined in
the Western Americana Collection of the Yale University
Library. Through the good offices of Archibald Hanna, the
Curator, the Department of History and the Library of Yale
University have granted me permission to publish the entire
text of the letters.

Allen Bogue, at the time a member of the History Department of the State University of Iowa, informed me of
the Eno letters deposited in the Special Collections of that
university library and in the Chicago Historical Society.
These manuscripts have provided invaluable information
on Henry's childhood, the difficulties he encountered as a
young lawyer in western New York, and particularly on the
Iowa years. Frank Paluka, Head of Special Collections, and
Jack King, Librarian of the State University of Iowa, have
generously granted permission for me to use these sources
in my introduction. My search for additional information

on the Iowa years of Eno's life has been skillfully guided
by Lida Lisle Greene, Librarian of the Iowa State Department of History and Archives in Des Moines, and by William J. Peterson, Marcelia Fisher, and others of the State
Historical Society of Iowa, Iowa City.

The activities of Edward, Henry's brother, in Illinois are
clearly depicted in his correspondence deposited at the
Chicago Historical Society. Archie Motley, Manuscript Librarian of the Chicago Historical Society, provided me with
photocopies. Additional material relating to Edward has
been forwarded by Clyde C. Walton, Illinois State Historical
Library, Springfield.

The staff of the Manuscripts and History Section of the
New York State Library in Albany made available an extensive collection of books and documents relating to
Stephen Eno, his son William, and their descendants. Moreover, they called my attention to county and local histories
and biographical works that otherwise would have been
overlooked.

The evidence I have obtained on the people and places
that were a part of Henry Eno's California has been gathered
in many California libraries, including the Bancroft Library
of the University of California, where George P. Hammond
the Director, John Barr Tomkins, Dale Morgan, and
Mrs. Julia H. Macleod have consistently come to my aid
through the years. James de T. Abajian of the California
Historical Society Library, San Francisco, and especially
Allan R. Ottley of the California State Library have spent
many hours seeking out and guiding me to the ephemeral
as well as the standard sources. My search for issues of the
Alpine County newspapers to which Henry Eno contributed
has been assisted by numerous individuals. In Nevada, for
example, officials in the State Library, Carson City, the Uni-

versity of Nevada Library and the Nevada Historical Society
in Reno, all gave of their time in an effort to procure isolated
issues. My colleague and friend Doyce B. Nunis, editor of
the *Southern California Quarterly,* has helped with advice
concerning the location of information on the last years of
Eno's life. My wife Barbara has made a major contribution
in checking the transcription of the manuscript into typescript and then into print with painstaking care, and has
maintained an enthusiasm for the publication project from
beginning to end that has been a source of encouragement
and inspiration.

W. T. J.

Davis, California
November 1964

NOTE

The letters have been printed as they appear in the manuscripts, with the exception of changes in Eno's punctuation
for the sake of clarity. His dashes used in place of commas,
semicolons, and periods have often been eliminated. Where an
end-of-sentence period has been added, it is followed by a
capital letter provided by the editor. Superscripts have been
brought down to the line. Repetitions of words, obvious mis-
spellings, and similar errors characteristic of long hand letters
have been left as Eno wrote them.

CONTENTS

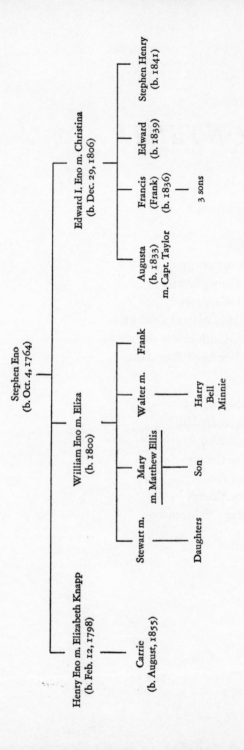

Stephen Eno
(b. Oct. 4, 1764)

Henry Eno m. Elizabeth Knapp
(b. Feb. 12, 1798)

William Eno m. Eliza
(b. 1800)

Edward I. Eno m. Christina
(b. Dec. 29, 1806)

Carrie
(b. August, 1855)

Stewart m.

Mary
m. Matthew Ellis

Walter m.

Frank

Augusta
(b. 1833)
m. Capt. Taylor

Francis
(Frank)
(b. 1836)

Edward
(b. 1839)

Stephen Henry
(b. 1841)

Daughters

Son

Harry
Bell
Minnie

3 sons

INTRODUCTION

HENRY ENO was an obscure man, an "everyman" who participated in the westward movement, and like most pioneers who migrated west he was an incurable optimist, a man in search of El Dorado. Arriving in California with the great horde of Forty-niners, he tried his ability as a lawyer, boardinghouse keeper, director of a water canal company, newspaperman, lecturer, and, above all, prospector for the ever-elusive precious metal, until he finally bade farewell to the Pacific Coast in 1871. Eno's life is representative of the many who believed in the right of every individual to pursue happiness as he envisioned it, coupled with a fundamental belief in the law of progress. Like many, he ran afoul of the laws of economics. Nevertheless, *nil desperandum* was his motto, and until the end he was certain that El Dorado was just over the next hill.

The pattern of Eno's life on the Pacific Slope was foreshadowed by events in his youth, early manhood in New York, and his sojourn in Iowa. The Eno family, of which he was a vital part, had its American roots in New York State. The patriarch of the family, Stephen, was born on October 4, 1764, in Simsbury, Connecticut, the second son in a family of five. In later years he recalled: "I spent my infant years (until ten years of age) at home in my father's house in Simsbury. Until that age I never went abroad out of the neighborhood, and was taught to read by my father at home, having no advantage of a school. I think I did not attend any kind of school, so much as a week till after this age, and I will here mention that in the whole course of my life I have never been to school two months."[1] Family poverty made it necessary for Stephen, at 10, to be sent to the home of an aunt at Egremont, Massachusetts, where he lived a life of hardship and despair for four or five years. As a lad of 17 he participated in the American Revolution on the patriot side and saw action on the Connecticut frontier near New Haven in 1781 and 1782.[2] When the war was over, he became an apprentice to a tanner in Cornwall, Connecticut, and remained there until he was 21. Self-educated, Stephen was greatly respected for his learning, and for the next six or seven years taught the fundamentals of reading and writing in various schools, usually in Amenia, New York. At 27 he began to read law as a clerk in the office of a young attorney in North East, New York. "My preceptor was very ill qualified for a teacher, and had but a scanty library, and did very little business," Stephen candidly stated in making his application to practice before the Supreme Court of New York some years later. "I verily believe he never spent two hours giving me any kind of instructions in his life and after the first two months I was scarce ever in his office. I kept school part of the time and pleaded cases before justices of the peace for a livelihood."[3]

1. Quoted in Isaac Huntting, *History of Little Nine Partners of North East Precinct, and Pine Plains, New York, Duchess County* (Amenia, N.Y., Chas. Walsh, 1897), p. 331. See also Henry Eno to William Eno, September 12, 1854, Western Americana Collection, Yale.

2. Edward Eno to William Eno, September 7, 1857, Yale. "I find in our father's journal that he was in the army at New Haven about the year 1781 or 2."

3. Huntting, p. 332. For additional biographical information, see James H. Smith, *History of Duchess County, New York: Illustrations and Biographical Sketches, Some of Its Prominent Men and Pioneers* (Syracuse, N.Y., D. Mason, 1882), p. 232.

In December 1795 Stephen married Mary Denton of Amenia. The next year he was licensed to practice as an attorney and counsellor-at-law in the Dutchess County Court of Common Pleas.[4] In these years he became recognized as a leader in the community, and on July 4, 1797, he was asked to deliver an address at the Independence Day celebration to an audience primarily of fellow veterans of the Revolution.[5] At Old Attlebury Corners, Stanford, on February 12, 1798, his eldest son was born, christened Henry but always affectionately called "Harry" by members of the family,[6] and late in 1800, William was born.[7]

Writing of his wife, Stephen noted: "She was prudent and industrious and after some time my business in law began to increase. I always lived and practiced in the county [Dutchess], in the towns of Amenia, Stanford, and North East." In 1803 he purchased a house and lot in Pine Plains and made that community his residence. Here on December 29, 1806, Edward, his third son, was born, when his father was 42 years of age.[8] Within the year Mary Eno died, at 38. Stephen later paid her tribute: "She was a lovely and excellent woman, and the twelve years which I lived with her were by far the happiest period in my life."[9] Among the material things Mary Eno left behind was a book of "Divine Songs, attempted in Easy Language, for the use of Children," published in 1797, on the inside cover of which was inscribed,

4. License issued on June 30, 1796, Stephen Eno Papers, New York State Library, Albany.

5. A manuscript copy of this address with Eno's editorial revisions, is filed in the Stephen Eno Papers, New York.

6. Henry Eno to William Eno, February 10, 1870, Yale. Twin girls, Phoebe and Eliza, had been the first born, but they died in infancy.

7. Ibid., June 22, 1865, Yale.

8. Edward Eno to Stephen Eno, December 27, 1847, Yale.

9. Quoted by Huntting, p. 333.

"Mary Eno's Book / Bought Dec. 4, 1799 / Mary Eno died September 5th, 1807 and gave this book to her son, William Eno."[10]

Following the death of Eno's wife the infant Edward was sent to live with female relatives, but the two older boys remained at the family home in Pine Plains and were cared for by housekeepers. Stephen made certain that the lads were educated. In 1810, when Henry was 12 and William 9, schoolmasters in the village of Pine Plains were employed to give them instruction. Three years later they were sent to nearby villages where they lived in boardinghouses and attended schools under recognized masters.[11] At 15 young Henry was attending school at Sharon Springs, New York, seventy-five miles from home. Letters to his family revealed the rigorous nature of education in the early nineteenth century. The scholars rose before six in the morning to attend prayers at the schoolhouse, and immediately thereafter all those who studied Latin recited a lesson in grammar. These exercises completed, breakfast was provided; and about an hour and a half after sunrise the young students received classroom instruction. Harry found the family

10. On June 30, 1866, William recorded, in the New Testament of the family, the epitaph on his mother's tombstone in the square of the town of Amenia: "Mary Eno wife of Stephen Eno who died September 5 1807 at 38 years / She was a fine and excellent woman." Both the New Testament and "Divine Songs" are in the Stephen Eno Papers, New York.

11. In his "Expense Book—General Household Account," three volumes of which remain, Eno kept a separate account identified as "Schooling," in which he recorded all payments made from 1810 to 1815 for education of his boys. Typical entries are: "Sept. 29, 1814 Paid Charles Hoag for schooling up to this day. Sent the money by Henry who says he paid it to the teacher. $5.55."; "William entered Mr. Perry's School May 15, 1815—and left it December 22, 1815 / The Certificate of Williams Schooling from David L. Perry is in the Pigeon Hole marked Miscellany."

where he boarded kind and obliging, and in time they provided a study room for the students they had taken in, so that
it would not be necessary for them to study at the schoolhouse after hours.[12] Apparently Henry had no feeling of
warmth or affection for his schoolmaster, for when he was
informed of the old man's death twenty-five years later, he
made the passing comment that he had lived so long in the
place, and his peculiarities had made him so well known,
that he presumed he would be missed.[13]

Meanwhile, Stephen Eno's law practice was expanding.
In 1803 he had been licensed to practice in the Court of
Common Pleas of Columbia County, and in 1810 he was
appointed Master in Chancery for the village of Pine Plains
in the heart of the township of North East. As he prospered,
Eno enlarged his residence, built a sizable barn, and in 1814
employed a master carpenter to erect an office building at
the cost of $300. The carpenter built well, for the structure
served Stephen throughout his lifetime and, after him, his
son William, then finally William's son.[14]

Stephen Eno's success did not go unchallenged, for a
group of neighbors on one occasion requested his removal as
Master in Chancery, claiming:

> Although licensed to practice in the higher courts yet
> his time is almost wholly employed among the petty
> disputes of his neighbors before single Justices of the
> peace. His talents his ingenuity and his knowledge of
> law instead of enlightening the path of Justice are too

12. Henry Eno to Stephen Eno, November 29, 1813, Special Collections, State University of Iowa Library, Iowa City. An item for
May 5, 1814, in the Expense Book reveals: "Paid for Henry's board and
tuition at Sharon for 6 months $62."

13. Henry Eno to Stephen Eno, September 15, 1838, Iowa.

14. Huntting, p. 334.

often successfully employed to mislead the sober honest judgment of the Justices of the peace before whom he practices and who unfortunately happen not to be so well versed in the laws as himself. Such conduct tends to the injury of morals to the perversion of justice, and much to the disadvantage of the good people of this vicinity.[15]

Perhaps more to the point, Eno was described as "a decided political enemy to the administration," and the rival lawyer whom they hoped to install was "uniformly a decided Republican." Nothing came of their charges, and Eno dismissed the matter as spite engendered by disappointed litigants. While his young sons were away at boarding school, Stephen married again, his second wife having been a harnessmaker in the village of Pine Plains. A son, Rufus, was born in 1816.[16]

Henry returned to Pine Plains to study law in his father's office and then worked under the supervision of Philip Parker, a well-known lawyer in Albany. He had completed reading in law by the age of 27, largely to please his father. Electing to initiate his practice in the county seat of one of the western New York counties, he left home, traveling up the Hudson River to Albany, by stage to Schenectady, then by freight boat and packet ship to Utica, and on to Syracuse, stopping repeatedly along the journey to collect loans his father had made to farmers and real estate speculators. But Henry was already more interested in collecting books than money and while in Albany purchased a basic law library on credit. In reporting this to his father, he noted, "it is as necessary for a lawyer to have books as it is for a soldier to

15. Manuscript petition in the Stephen Eno Papers, New York.
16. Huntting, p. 334.

have a musket."[17] Although his father thought he had been somewhat extravagant in buying $150 worth of law books, he later assisted him by forwarding $50 to reduce the debt.[18]

Henry took up residence in Penn Yan, county seat of Yates County.[19] The next three years of his life were typical of those of a struggling young lawyer. He sought out and presented himself to the judge of the Court of Common Pleas, who in turn introduced him to other members of the bar and invited him to call at his office and use the books in his library. Next Henry made a tour of every town in the county to get acquainted. Business was trifling, and the necessity to economize forced him to leave the tavern opposite the courthouse where his board was $2 a week and take up lodging in a cheaper rooming house. He had hopes of being appointed district attorney within a year but was disappointed. During dull times in 1826 he read chancery books in order to qualify as a solicitor, volunteered to fight fires in Penn Yan, and traveled about the state from Cayuga to Poughkeepsie. He filed an application for the office of surrogate which proved unsuccessful, but was given a consolation post as Master of Chancery, which in turn led to his qualifying and being licensed as a solicitor in chancery. All these negotiations meant trips to Albany (where he was able to meet his brother William, who had also obtained a license as attorney and counsellor in the Court of Common Pleas in Dutchess County) to buy books at auctions and talk with politicians who could advance his career.[20]

17. Henry Eno to Stephen Eno, September [?], 1825. The Eno correspondence cited in notes 17 through 19 is in the Iowa collection.

18. Ibid., December 8, 1825.

19. Ibid., October 2, 1825.

20. Ibid., January 29, April 19, August 14, December 28, 1826, April 29, September 17, 1827; Iowa. License of William Eno to practice in the Dutchess County Court of Common Pleas, April 1823, Stephen

While Henry seemed restless, William had elected to keep his base of operations in Dutchess County, with occasional trips to the capital, and was prospering in his profession, accumulating agricultural and timber lands, and eventually became an investor in banks and railroads after his retirement from legal practice. He husbanded his father's resources and provided the financial assistance to tide the other members of the family over periodic crises.[21]

Just as Henry's career began to blossom, he developed a fondness for alcohol that was to plague him periodically throughout his life and bring him close to self-destruction. For five years, as an alcoholic, he failed to communicate with his father, for whom he had always demonstrated the greatest affection and respect. At last, in October 1832, he took up his pen to write an apologia.

> How to address myself to the kindest of parents I scarcely know—or how I can hope to be forgiven for treating with neglect and a seeming want of affection my father for whom of all persons on earth my duty & love were most owing—Nothing but an infatuation for which I cannot account joined with some misfortunes which I am sorry to say I had not at the time

---

Eno Papers, New York. In addition to being trained in law William was also an accomplished surveyor, who made an elaborate, detailed map of the village of Pine Plains and the surrounding area in 1821. Copy in the Stephen Eno Papers, New York.

21. In February 1826 William was licensed to practice in the New York State Supreme Court and in August 1834 to serve as solicitor and counsellor in the New York State Court of Chancery. He maintained a law office in Pine Plains and profited from the advice of his father relative to cases tried before the Poughkeepsie courts. He was appointed attorney for Dutchess County for two terms, was elected to the state legislature in 1836, and was supervisor for several terms. Huntting, p. 334. Licenses in the Stephen Eno Papers, New York.

strength of mind to surmount could have led me to be guilty of conduct which I cannot help but call criminal ... If I thought you could forgive me it would remove almost the only painful thorn now rankling in my bosom—I wish to return & see the land where my boyhood was spent & to see my father & brothers who I believe love me still notwithstanding all my faults—but I cannot return until I can carry with me some convincing proof that I am worthy to be called your son ... I am treated in this place with all the respect that any one is & shall in future attempt not only to deserve but preserve it—Again I say father forgive me and you *shall* have occasion to be proud of your son.[22]

During the next three years, conscious of self-degradation and knowing that he had disappointed the fond hopes of his father, Henry penitently attempted to reorder his life. A former member of the New York Assembly offered to provide him with a law library, another lawyer in the village invited him to form a partnership, and he also received an offer to go to Cincinnati, Ohio, with all expense of removal paid, to edit a newspaper.[23] Within a year he had indeed acquired a library, had formed a partnership with a younger lawyer, and had commenced seven cases to go before the New York Supreme Court. In response to his father's pleas to come home, he insisted that he must remain in Penn Yan to work industriously at his business for "being in debt I consider worse than Egyptian bondage, & like the children of Israel I intend soon to break the fetters."[24] Meanwhile, he expressed appreciation to his father for encouraging him

22. Henry Eno to Stephen Eno, October 30, 1832. The Eno correspondence cited in notes 22 through 52 is in the Iowa collection.

23. Ibid., November 9, 1832.

24. Ibid., April 10, 1833.

to read good literature in his youth, as he was able to beguile the hours that hung heavy on his hands "in conversation with books" and was also enabled to write articles for the regional newspapers. While pleading a case before the court, he made a sensational proposal that the judges and members of the bar should form a temperance society in accordance with the recommendations of the Chief Justice of the New York Supreme Court. The upshot of his proposal was an organizational meeting at which Henry was elected secretary.

On September 20, 1832, Henry's brother Edward married a young lady by the name of Christina, and Henry observed that he had allied himself with a very good family and would look out well for himself. The next year Edward joined a New York firm of merchants and was sent to New Bedford, Massachusetts, a town which he and Christina contrasted unfavorably with their former New York home, Kinderhook. "This is a *monied* place is about all I can say in its favour. The inhabitants have gained most of their wealth by *Fishing*—the *Whale* fishing is carried on verry extensively and has been the means of making many of those employed immensely rich. They understand their business well, but farther than that their information is limited. . . . This place labours under the disadvantage of having a verry rough barren County round it, consequently the meat & vegatable market is verry poor and what there is is high."[25] Edward also reported in June 1833 that he had received the one and only letter from Henry since he left home, in which he asked the family not to judge him too harshly, expressed regrets for the past, admitted that he was poor and never expected to be wealthy, but that he intended

25. Edward Eno to Stephen Eno, June 5, 1833.

to remain in Penn Yan until he had paid his debts, perhaps longer.[26]

During these trying years Henry Eno revealed an abiding concern and pride in his brothers. He confided to his father that everyone who came to Yates County from the East spoke highly of William and reported that he was doing well. In March 1834 William had forwarded $500 to Henry to pay off all his creditors to avoid legal action against him and to free his mind from the perplexities and cares that harassed him.[27] When William went to Albany to become licensed as a solicitor and counsellor in Chancery, Henry congratulated him on entering a wider field and displaying the energy that had taken him to the top in the profession.[28] Henry also took time to write a letter to William's boy, Stewart, not certain that he had yet learned to read but in hopes of exciting his ambition. He noted that impressions received early in life were the most lasting, and it was never too early to begin the lad's education. In particular, he recommended that *Parley's Magazine,* selling for one dollar a year, should be purchased for Master Stewart, for it would "learn him a great deal."

Through the years Henry continued to express concern over his half-brother Rufus. When he left for western New York to take up the practice of law, Henry had urged the young lad to write him as a means of improving his penmanship and had encouraged him to be a dutiful scholar. In his darkest hours of rehabilitation Henry thought of Rufus, expressing the hope that he intended to become an industrious farmer.[29] When the young man sent him a

26. Ibid.
27. Henry Eno to Stephen Eno, March 13, 1834.
28. Ibid., March 26, September 3, 1834.
29. Ibid., March 13, 1834.

survey map he had made of a neighboring farm, Henry again urged him to combine surveying with farming, "the noblest employment" and the surest road to health and wealth.[30] Stephen was forced to tell Henry in September 1834 that Rufus was "an unpromising boy" who spent his time with those interested in raising and racing horses. Henry recommended that his father purchase an interest in a farm for the errant lad, so that he could acquire something to call his own and at the same time have business that occupied his entire attention. For a time Henry considered inviting Rufus to attend the academy in Penn Yan and work in his law office, but finally concluded that if he had a disinclination to study coupled with an inclination to keep bad company, the village was the wrong place for him.[31] Nothing seemed to spur Rufus into enterprise, and a year later Henry again expressed anxiety and urged his father to find some kind of employment that would keep him from idleness.

Business was uncommonly slow for lawyers in western New York in 1834 because of the limited money supply and the low prices prevailing for farmers' products. During a "farming mania" the previous year good agricultural land sold on credit for as high as $40 an acre. Many of the purchasers were desperately trying to meet their payments at a time when their income from wheat, rye, and corn was greatly reduced and borrowing was next to impossible. As land values fell 25 per cent, those who had money to lend could obtain 25 per cent interest on good security. Moreover, the country was overrun with lawyers. Henry reported that he had his share of the legal business of the county, but

30. Ibid., March 26, 1834.
31. Ibid., September 3, 1834.

that it consisted of only five minor cases. To fill his time, he turned to politics and was elected delegate to the nominating convention at Seneca Falls to designate a senatorial candidate. Early in 1835 he made a trip to Albany and successfully defended a colleague who was on the verge of being disbarred for malpractice. When summer came, he went home to visit his father and brother William for the first time in ten years.[32]

In February 1836 Henry announced his determination to leave western New York. Although he would be leaving family and friends behind, he was convinced that the profession of law would never make him rich, and he wanted to go to the western states, where he could combine land speculations with his legal practice. Like many other men who joined the mass migration from New England and New York into the states of the Old Northwest in this decade, Henry was convinced that he had everything to gain and nothing to lose. In addition to the basic motive of economic improvement, he wanted to leave Yates County and the memories associated with the area, for "it will be to me like publishing as Franklin says a new edition of life—I shall have the opportunity in one of our western cities of correcting the errors of the first edition."[33] Henry had chosen Peoria on the Illinois River for his destination; the town was booming, and some thought it would become the capital of the state. In notifying his father of his intention to become a "western man," he reminded him that Edward was now in business in New York and William was a respected lawyer in Albany. Henry traveled to Albany to obtain letters of recommendation from men of influence that would assist

32. Ibid., March 26, April 23, June 20, September 3, October 7, 1834, January 20, July 11, October 4, 1835.
33. Ibid., February 14, 1836.

him where he was going, including one from the Governor
of New York introducing him to the Governor of Illinois.
When spring came, Henry sold his worldly goods on credit
and forwarded the promissory notes and a mortgage on his
real estate to his father, who returned the cash necessary to
make the move west. Rather than go to Illinois with a
wagon train, as planned, he decided at the last minute to
accompany a young heir to Toledo, Ohio, and assist him in
settling his inheritance, also hoping thereby to pay his own
removal expenses. At this juncture he anticipated working
in Illinois for five years and, if unsuccessful, trying elsewhere.[34]

Stopping in Peoria briefly, Henry headed west to Fort
Madison, on the west bank of the Mississippi River and in
1837 still a part of Wisconsin Territory. He was the town's
first citizen trained in law.[35] In general, the laws of Michigan
were recognized, with the exception of a few specific modi-
fications prescribed by the Wisconsin territorial legislature.
As the Michigan code was based upon that of New York,
Eno was convinced that he would feel more at home and
more effective in practicing law here than in Illinois. In accordance with the judicial system for the western territories,
Wisconsin had been divided into three judicial districts,
each of the judges being appointed by the President of the
United States. One of these districts comprised the land west
of the Mississippi River. It, in turn, was divided into six
county units, in which the territorial district court convened
twice a year, the judge traveling on circuit. Henry Eno met

34. Ibid., April 3, 26, 1836.
35. *The History of Lee County, Iowa* (Chicago, Western Historical
Co., 1879), p. 543. Edward H. Stiles, *Recollections and Sketches of
Notable Lawyers and Public Men in Early Iowa* (Des Moines, Homestead Publishing Co., 1916), p. 324.

the judge and told him of his plans to accompany the court, expecting to get professional work in each place the court convened. Lawyers were few on this frontier in 1837, and citizens were accustomed to paying high prices for their services. This first trip lasted six weeks, from March to April of 1837, and Henry made many new acquaintances. In addition, he was speculating in lands, having purchased for $200 a claim of 240 acres with a log cabin on it, about a mile and a half outside of Fort Madison. The land had not yet been officially surveyed and placed on the market by the federal government. However, pioneers were accustomed to organizing claims associations to protect the lands acquired by settlers prior to the arrival of the government surveyor. Nowhere were settlers more certain that their land rights would be respected—that no late-comer would be permitted to outbid the pre-emptor when their acreage was auctioned by the government—than in this region west of the Mississippi River. Once Henry got his patent, he expected to hold the property for five years, at which time he anticipated its value would have increased fiftyfold. In Dutchess County, New York, similar land, he thought, would bring $100 an acre.[36]

Eno explained in letters to his relatives that Burlington, twenty miles from Fort Madison on the banks of the Mississippi River, was the temporary seat of government and contained about 800 inhabitants. Fort Madison, twenty miles north of the mouth of the Des Moines River, had 400. Twelve miles below was Fort Des Moines, where two companies of dragoons were stationed. Black Hawk had his wickiup, or cabin, six miles south of the town, but Henry was of the opinion that "there is no more danger to be ap-

36. Henry Eno to Stephen Eno, March 11, 1837.

prehended from Indians than there is from the Dutch in
Columbia Co." He loved his new home.

> In beauty of situation Fort Madison will compare with
> any place I have seen in the far west except Peoria—it
> has the advantage over Peoria in the broad Mississippi
> and is I should think a healthier location—the char-
> acter of the population is not of that lawless character
> which is imagined at the east—& for what I can at
> present see there is as much morality and honesty
> among the settlers as in the same number of persons in
> New York—many of the emigrants are from New
> York & the Eastern States and they bring with them
> their manners habits & customs—the coming spring
> and summer will add greatly to the population in the
> region—it is now estimated at 10000 west of the river
> & in 1832 there was scarcely a white man between
> the Ioway & the Des Moines—the Winter has been
> unusually cold but the river is now breaking up &
> steamboats are expected in the course of a week—last
> year there were fifteen steamboats engaged in the trade
> on the Upper Mississippi—it is said there will be more
> this year—[37]

Henry rode on horseback fifty miles west to the Des Moines
River, at the Indian boundary, and then traveled down that
stream to its mouth. He thought there was not a more
handsome stream in the far west or better land that bordered
it. The government surveyors were in the process of surveying the sections, and when the land came on the market Eno
had chosen the acreage he wanted.

As the Panic of 1837 gripped the eastern states bringing

37. Ibid.

about the bankruptcy of business houses and the closing of banks, Eno reported that the money shortage did not seriously affect the trans-Mississippi country, where there were no banks and the liabilities of merchants were minimal. Newly arrived settlers—at least 3,000 had crossed the river at Fort Madison between May and July of 1837—brought cash with them sufficient for their initial needs and thereby augmented the money supply. There was now talk that a new territory would be created by 1840.

Meanwhile, William and Edward were having difficulty adjusting to the depression. William remained solvent, and for a while it appeared that Edward would also weather the storm; but then news came that his business had failed. Henry advised him not to come West to get a new start, for the country was full of merchants and speculators in lands, most of whom were not successful.

When July 4, 1837, arrived, Henry was called upon to give an open air "western style" speech to 500 "Iowa" citizens, after which the assemblage ate dinner in a forest grove near the town. In his leisure he began reading the discourses of Cicero, which he recommended to young and old alike, and already was developing a philosophical outlook on life, admitting to relatives that although he had arrived at an age where the buoyancy of youth had departed, he no longer had any anxiety about growing old. In fact, he thought himself happier and more content between 30 and 40 than he had been between 20 and 30.[38]

While practicing his profession, Eno became active in public affairs, taking a leading part in the movement to divide the Territory of Wisconsin and organize a separate Territory of Iowa. He personally drew up the following

38. Ibid., July 12, 1837.

call for a meeting of citizens to prepare a petition to Congress:

COUNTY MEETING

A County Meeting will be held at the house of C. L. Cope, in the town of Fort Madison, on Saturday, the fourteenth of October, next, at one o'clock, p.m., for the purpose of choosing three delegates to meet in Convention at Burlington on the first Monday of November, next, to take into consideration the expediency of petitioning Congress for a division of the Territory of Wisconsin, and the organization of a separate Territorial Government west of the Mississippi. Also the attempt making by the State of Missouri to extend her northern boundary line, and to call the attention of Congress to the necessity of granting preemption laws to actual settlers, and for other purposes.

Dated September 23d, 1837[39]

Eno was elected as one of the three delegates to represent Lee County at the Burlington convention that assembled on November 6. The next day, when the thirty-odd delegates gathered, he moved that a committee of seven be appointed by the president of the convention to draft a memorial to Congress on the subject of the attempt of the State of Missouri to extend its northern boundary, and was immediately named chairman of such a committee. Some years earlier commissioners appointed by the State of Missouri had drawn a northern boundary line for the state that crossed the Des Moines River at a point approximately twenty-four

39. Hawkins Taylor, "Before and after the Territorial Organization of Iowa," *Annals of Iowa,* 1st ser. 9 (January 1871), 455.

miles from its mouth; and when the line was continued directly eastward, it struck the Mississippi River just south of the town of Fort Madison. Prior to the meeting of this Burlington convention the Missouri legislature had appointed a new group of commissioners to relocate the boundary, and they selected a point on the Des Moines River twelve or fourteen miles farther north. If this line were extended eastward it would strike the Mississippi River at Burlington and, what was of immediate concern to Henry Eno, place his home town of Fort Madison in the State of Missouri rather than in the Wisconsin Territory or in the proposed new Iowa Territory. The memorial, as unanimously approved, urged Congress to take immediate action appointing commissioners to run the boundary line between the State of Missouri and the Territory of Wisconsin according to the spirit and intention of the act of June 1820, which established Missouri.[40]

Iowa Territory was created on July 4, 1838, and Eno observed: "The division of the Territory pleases every one I believe and Gove Lucas the ex Gove of Ohio also pleases the people   he is a man about 65 years old, very plain, but appears to be a strong minded man—"[41] The territorial legislature consisted of thirteen council members and twenty-six members of the assembly. Eno was nominated by a convention to run for the council, but he withdrew from the race because he anticipated an appointment from the Governor

---

40. The proceedings and all memorials adopted by the Burlington Convention were printed in pamphlet form and transmitted to Congress. The entire text was printed in the Dubuque *Iowa News, 1,* November 24, 1837. Some years later the documents were reprinted in the *Iowa Journal of History and Politics,* 9 (1911), 394–401.

41. Henry Eno to Stephen Eno, September 15, 1838. The act creating the Territory of Iowa was signed by President Van Buren on June 12, 1838, to take effect on July 4.

to the commission that was to run the boundary line between
Iowa and Missouri. After other men were chosen, Eno called
on the Governor, who expressed regret, asserting that he
did not know Eno wished the appointment. Henry admitted
to his father that he had declined to run even though there
was no doubt he would be elected, but that he did not regret
the decision; the time had come for him to attend to his
own business rather than that of the "dear people."[42] This
was a pose, for soon he was drafting a memorial to Congress
praying for federal aid in the construction of a railroad
from Fort Madison westward sixty-five miles by way of the
town of West Point to the point where the Indian boundary
line crossed the Des Moines River. Without question, Henry
Eno was already recognized by his peers and the members
of the territorial legislature as having exceptional talent in
writing the English language. He argued his case as follows:

> Its great value and importance to the country through
> which it would pass is deemed unnecessary to detail
> at length. It would afford a channel through which the
> products of the industry of an enterprising, hardy, and
> numerous population would be sent to the Mississippi.
> It would enhance the value of the lands through which
> it would run, and afford quick and ready communica-
> tion over a fertile country through which there are now
> no good roads. It would give additional value to govern-

42. Dubuque *Iowa News, 1,* May 26, 1838; Louis Pelzer, "The History and Principles of the Democratic Party in the Territory of Iowa,"
Iowa Journal of History and Politics, 6 (1908), 9–10. Pelzer suggests
that Henry Eno was a Democrat and announced his candidacy for the
council after an enthusiastic meeting of the members of the party. Eno
himself always claimed to be a Whig even though his loyalty to this
minority party in Iowa and California hindered his chances of election.
Events subsequent to the nominating convention are revealed in a
letter from Henry Eno to Stephen Eno, September 15, 1838.

ment lands . . . But, aside from the great and manifest
utility to the whole country through which the road
would pass, your memorialists deem it of paramount
importance to provide in time of peace for the safety
and defense of thousands of American citizens who are
now residing in a land contiguous to large and numerous bodies of Indians. . . . It would facilitate the supplying and relief of a military post now erecting by government at or near the Raccoon Forks of the Des Moines
river, and would contribute materially to keeping the
Indians in awe, and securing the peace and tranquility
of our frontier. Your memorialists, therefore, pray for
the appointment of an engineer to survey the above
route, and for such a donation of public land as will
enable the Territory of Iowa to complete the work.[43]

With the creation of the Territory it became necessary
to appoint all officials again, and Eno was not certain that
he would be reappointed Judge of Probate. The office had
not proved profitable in the two years he had held it but
would be in the future. Apparently he remained on good
terms with Governor Robert Lucas, for in January 1839 the
Governor did ask the council of the territorial assembly to
designate him Judge of Probate in Lee County.[44]

Many Iowa residents were concerned about the action of

43. This memorial was published in full by Hawkins Taylor in "Early
Men and Early Days Recalled," *Annals of Iowa*, 1st ser. 10 (January
1872), 26. Taylor says that Eno was a member of the territorial legislature in 1838 and 1839 when he drafted this memorial. The official
journals do not list Eno as a member so it appears that Taylor's memory
was false. Eno may well have drafted the memorial to Congress at the
request of a committee in the legislature.

44. B. F. Shambaugh, ed., *Executive Journal of Iowa, 1838–1841*,
p. 83.

Congress in June 1838 allowing pre-emption rights to settlers, because the law provided, among other things, that
they must have been in residence on the claim for four
months prior to the passage of the law. Eno was among the
many who could not qualify for all the acreage he had accumulated. However, he was certain he could purchase his
land at the minimum price, through cooperation with the
Claims Protective Association. The President's proclamation
implementing the law had brought about fifty Iowa townships on the market, twenty-five of which were in the land
district that included Eno's home county of Lee. The acreage
was to go on sale at the land office in Burlington on November 19, 1838, and before that date all entitled to pre-emption rights had to take them up. Upon inquiry, Eno learned
that three townships in Lee County would be thrown on the
market, but the one in which his 240-acre claim was located
was not included. He anticipated that it would certainly
come on the market in the spring of 1839. He had been
granted a reprieve, for he did not have the money to pay
for his holding.[45]

Eno and his business associates were also authorized by
the territorial legislature to construct a mill dam across the
Des Moines River at Bentonsport in Van Buren County.[46]
At this time freighting by keel boat was the chief means of
bringing in supplies to the towns along the river, and the
American Fur Company frequently made shipments to its
trading posts up the river by small steamboats. In order not
to interfere with this river traffic, the law required that dams
be not more than three feet above the low-water mark and
contain convenient locks not less than 130 feet in length and
35 feet in width, so that steam, keel, flatboats, rafts, and

45. Henry Eno to Stephen Eno, September 15, 1838.
46. Shambaugh, p. 292.

other water craft could navigate the river.[47] Undoubtedly
Eno and his partners planned to construct a mill or to dispose
of the site for that purpose.

Eno's professional activities and his public service made
him a well-known and respected member of Iowa society,
but he was not neglecting his personal affairs. On March 14,
1838, he married Elizabeth Knapp.[48] His marriage had
been delayed until his fortieth year, possibly because of a
lengthy struggle for financial security and professional success. Elizabeth was the daughter of General John A. Knapp,
from New York State, who had arrived west of the Mississippi River in the summer of 1833 when that area was
still a part of the Michigan Territory, prior to its transfer to
Wisconsin. The General was among those who laid out the
town of Fort Madison on the banks of the River. Henry
reported his change of status to his father:

> Since I last wrote you I have left the *Territory* of Single
> Blessedness & entered into the *State* of Wedlock—I
> know this news will surprise you and am rather afraid
> that you will not be pleased with it—as you will prob-
> ably think I was too old a Batchelor to think of altering
> my situation—The girl I have married I have been
> acquainted with for about four years & a half—she is
> sixteen years younger than I am & is the youngest
> daughter of the late Gen John H. Knapp who first
> settled this town & was formerly from Tioga Co N.Y.

47. Jacob Van der Zee, "The Opening of the Des Moines Valley,"
Iowa Journal of History and Politics, 14 (1916), 553–54. Van der Zee
has traced the legislation on this subject in the *Laws of the Territory of
Iowa, 1838–1839, 1840–1841, 1842–1843.*

48. Vital Statistics of Lee County pioneers, compiled by the Daughters of the American Revolution, Iowa State Department of History and
Archives, Des Moines.

—her name is Elizabeth—This was no hasty thoughtless act of mine for with me the romance of Youth is
over and gone I wished to have a home I could call my
own to settle down & have some one at my fireside who
was not a stranger—for here I had no relative of any
kind nearer than a thousand miles and of course must
feel at times lonely enough—Elizabeth has been
brought up to industrious habits is of a domestic turn
& I believe of a good temper and disposition—If the
old maxim is correct—to chose the daughter of a good
mother—I have made a good choice—but that time
alone will determine—It would give me much pleasure
to have your approval & would you write her a letter
        it would please us both—I hope to be able next
year to bring her to New York and to see you in good
health & to have you welcome her as another daughter
added to your family—[49]

The newlyweds, Elizabeth and Henry, established themselves in the one-room log cabin on the acreage outside
Fort Madison, in what Henry thought was a "delightful
situation," with a good well of water, a garden, and fifty
acres of hardwood timber. According to the census of 1840
the household consisted of one female between 20 and 30,
one male between 30 and 40, and one male between 15 and
20.[50] Apparently Henry was fudging a bit on his age, for
at this date he should have been 42. The second male in the
family was Elizabeth's youngest brother, who made his

49. Henry Eno to Stephen Eno, March 29, 1838.
50. Census of Iowa Territory, 1840, Lee County, Fort Madison,
p. 371. This census has been microfilmed at the National Archives and
is available at the State Historical Society of Iowa, Iowa City.

home with the couple.[51] Henry maintained a law office in
town and walked to work every day. He planned to move
into town for the winter of 1839–40, but to return to his
country cabin in the spring and improve it so he and Elizabeth could reside there permanently.

During this period the temperance movement was very
strong in the Iowa Territory, and on April 27, 1838, a new
society was organized in Fort Madison, with fifty members,
of which Henry Eno was vice-president, pledged to dis-
courage the use, manufacture, and sale of intoxicating
liquors as a beverage.[52] Henry maintained a continuous interest in the temperance movement. On December 27, 1848,
he met with thirteen fellow citizens to organize a division
of the national Sons of Temperance, and within the week
123 members were enrolled.[53]

In 1838 news arrived from New York that Rufus had
left the Eno family home without Stephen's consent. Henry
was fearful that the course he had adopted would ruin his
life.[54] When the prodigal returned home, Henry wrote his
father proposing that the young man be sent out to Iowa.
He suggested that there was less intemperance and temptation to vice on the frontier than in Dutchess County, New
York. Henry's plan was for his father to purchase 160 acres
of land for Rufus at the minimum government price and
spend an additional $150 to erect a cabin on it and plough
up ten acres for farming. If Rufus worked at improving the

51. Henry Eno to Stephen Eno, September 15, 1838. General Knapp
had died in January 1836 leaving two daughters and three sons, not
just two as Eno wrote.

52. *The Fort Madison Patriot, 1,* May 2, 1838; Dan Elbert Clark,
"The Beginnings of Liquor Legislation in Iowa," *Iowa Journal of History and Politics,* 5 (1907), 196–97.

53. Henry Eno to William Eno, December 31, 1848, Yale.

54. Henry Eno to Stephen Eno, September 15, 1838, Iowa.

land, Henry thought his father might convey the title to him at the end of two years.[55] Stephen, however, elected to turn to Edward rather than Henry. Once the Panic of 1837 had passed, Edward formed a partnership in New York City to engage in merchandising, chiefly hardware, and was sanguine of success. He had kept in close touch with his father, for periodically he had to ask for a temporary loan of cash to preserve his credit rating. When Stephen asked him to find a place for Rufus in his business, Edward refused, on the grounds that without experience and capital to sustain himself for the first three years the young man could not hope to succeed in the New York trade.[56] Rufus apparently never found his place in society, and by 1845 he was dead.[57]

Henry had problems of his own. Although his marriage was a happy one, his wife Elizabeth was chronically ill. Income from his law practice was minimal. Members of the legal profession in Iowa had increased so rapidly between 1837 and 1839 that there was insufficient business to go around, and lawyers were taking cases on a commission rather than a fee basis. At times, Eno considered giving up his practice to engage in farming. Meanwhile, he continued to deal in real estate. Suddenly, in the summer of 1839, he realized that he was $900 in debt and unable to convert his property into cash to advantage. The scarcity of money had driven interest rates to 25 per cent, although the law per-

55. Ibid., November 29, 1838, Iowa.
56. Edward Eno to Stephen Eno, October 16, 1839, Yale.
57. Ibid., December 29, 1845, Iowa. The General Household Account Books of Stephen Eno reveal that the second Mrs. Eno did not remain long as supervisor of the home, for in 1824 Stephen was paying William's wife, Eliza Ann, weekly wages for her service in this capacity. This arrangement lasted until William and Eliza established a separate household, and then Rose Eno, a cousin, came to live at the homestead in Pine Plains. During July and August of 1845 both Rose and Rufus

mitted only a maximum of 20 per cent when recorded in a contract. Moreover, he realized that his original 240-acre tract was coming on the market in October 1839 and that he desperately needed the money to purchase it. In anxiety he wrote his brother William and asked to borrow $1,500 for a single year at 10 per cent interest, giving a mortgage on all his Iowa real estate. He apologized for making the request, realizing that William had already come to Edward's assistance following the Panic of 1837 and that he was financially responsible for a growing family.[58] Henry also wrote to his father in the late summer, urging him to coun-

------

became ill, possibly with a contagious disease. The meticulous account books for the week of August 4–11, 1845, suggest what transpired and reveal the character and personality of Stephen Eno:

Aug. 4	Paid Samuel J. Spencer for attending upon Rufus $	5.
	Paid Mrs. Simmons for washing	0.35
5	B's store for 1 lb. Spermasetta [spermaceti] candles	0.44
6	Paid for cloth for Rufus's shroud	2.25
7	Paid Samuel J. Spencer for attending upon Rufus in his last sickness—16 days in the whole, $1 a day	16.00
	Paid for a bottle of wild cherry tree bark for Rose	1.00
	Paid Elutus B. Chamberlain for coffin for Rufus	12.00
	Gave to Wm. Breed for his services in attending the funeral of Rufus Eno	5.00
8	D & A for 3¾ lb. beef at 5	0.18
	Paid Q. Bunnel for a bottle of Dr. Janes Carminative	0.56
	Paid John Kilmer for whitewash & lime	0.87½
9	Paid J.J.N. Davis, for visits and medicine for Rose Eno	2.50
	Paid J.J.N. Davis, for visits and attendance upon Rufus Eno	35.62½
11	Paid Mrs. Simmons for washing	0.31

58. Henry Eno to William Eno, August 1, 1839. The Eno correspondence cited in notes 58 through 71 is in the Iowa collection.

sel with William about advancing him the needed cash so
he could hold on to his real estate. "I have no reason to
complain of fortune," he added, "my present situation is far
better than it was a few years ago . . . I have weathered
harder gales than will blow this season."[59]

But the gale soon blew that left Henry prostrate. In
August 1839 he was seized by a violent attack of "bilious
fever" accompanied by headaches. For five days and nights
he knew no one. On the twelfth day his fever turned down-
ward, but in a fortnight he had a relapse more acute than
the first attack. The hair was shaved from his head and his
weight dropped from a normal 168 pounds to 130. While
recuperating, he suffered an attack of mumps. This left him
with a desperate inflammation of the eyes, and he was confined for several weeks to a dark room.[60] The session of
the District Court was held, and Henry was unable to attend
to the forty-odd cases in which he was to be engaged. For
some months he accepted his plight philosophically and
wrote relatives that he was not depressed in spirits but thankful that he was as well off as he was.[61] He maintained his
courage even though admitting he had done no business of
any kind, nor earned a dollar for an entire year.

When his eyes failed, he and Elizabeth moved into her
sister's home.[62] Impoverished and unable to pay the interest
on loans made by his brother William and from his wife's
estate, he began to sell his real estate for what it would
bring. He also seemed unable to meet the competition of
his profession and complained that even though Iowa and

59. Henry Eno to Stephen Eno, August 2, 1839.
60. Ibid., October 20, 1839, August 1, 1840; Henry Eno to William
Eno, October 17, 1840.
61. Henry Eno to Stephen Eno, October 20, 1839.
62. Ibid., August 1, 1840.

Dutchess County were equal in population, there were five times as many lawyers in Iowa. Money was still bringing from 20 to 50 per cent annual interest. Since the law permitted charging as high as 20 per cent, he felt certain he could become a successful agent for an eastern capitalist. His spirits reached an all-time low in October 1840, however, when he wrote: "I really feel now as if all my fond hopes of an honest independence had been blasted, but as I have always been poor I can still bear it, altho at my time of life and the state of my health it is harder for me than ever—"[63]

Somehow Henry managed to renew his law practice. In 1841 he appeared before the courts not only in Lee County but in adjoining Van Buren County.[64] He still continued to move about with the territorial judge on circuit to plead for various clients. It was a strenuous life on occasions; court procedures in early day Iowa were rough and tumble affairs. For example, the justice of the peace in Fort Madison was no friend of the rowdies, and one "big, rough, drunken, dangerous fellow" threatened a physical encounter when the judge refused to grant him lodging and board in the local jail. Thus threatened, the justice of the peace took a hickory club and beat the man on the head until he was cut, bruised, and bloody. The justice was quickly arrested for assault and battery, and in a trial that lasted several days Eno defended him against the bitterness of his enemies. Eno won the case, the roughs learned that the judge meant business, and Fort Madison became more orderly.[65]

63. Henry Eno to William Eno, October 17, 1840.
64. "The Writing of Judge George G. Wright," *Annals of Iowa*, 3rd ser. 11 (January 1915), 598.
65. Hawkins Taylor, "Law Ministers of the Olden Time," *Annals of Iowa*, 1st ser. 9 (July 1871), 606–13. See also "The Early Bar of Lee County," *Annals of Iowa*, 1st ser. 9 (July 1871), 613–16.

Eno also maintained an interest in public affairs. The Wisconsin legislature in January 1838 had designated Fort Madison as the county seat of Lee County, but the second territorial legislature of Iowa, 1839–40, reopened the question under pressure and appointed a commission to choose a more centrally located site. This action resulted in a temporary removal of the county government to the town of Franklin. Popular protest forced the next session of the Iowa legislature to refer the issue to the people in an election. Eno was among a group of Fort Madison citizens who signed a bond underwriting a guarantee of the president and trustees of the town to appropriate $8,000 for public buildings, including a courthouse and jail, if the county seat were returned. The first election in March 1841 ended with none of the aspiring communities having a clear majority, but in the second election a month later Fort Madison was victorious.[66]

In 1843 Elizabeth and Henry went back to New York to visit relatives and friends. The Enos had a difficult time trying to decide whether to remain or to return to Iowa. A primary consideration was that Elizabeth, continuously sick, seemed to improve under the care of a New York physician. In addition, Elizabeth's uncle died at his home in Oxford, New York, and Henry was needed to settle the estate, in which her mother was the primary beneficiary. Although Henry had made inquiries about legal work in New York City and had been promised employment, he knew that their remaining real estate in the town of Fort Madison was steadily appreciating, and, still feeling that the western states were the land of opportunity, finally decided to return to Iowa in 1845 after settling the estate.[67]

66. *History of Lee County,* pp. 78–83, 443–45, 459–60.
67. Henry Eno to Stephen Eno, October 25, 1843.

The next year Henry was exchanging parcels of real estate, hoping to make sufficient profit to pay off the heavy indebtedness to his brother William, retire the mortgages, and hold property in his own name. His interest in public affairs temporarily waned, for he wrote: "I could have received a nomination to Congress this fall but I knew I should not be elected [delegate] & I also knew it would cost more dimes than I have or could muster to stand the canvass—so I gave it the *go by* and am glad of it. Who will be United States Senators from the New State is now the absorbing question. There are about one hundred and fifty men in the New State who think themselves entitled to the station and eminently qualified to fill it. Mr. Eno's chance is about as good if he had a ticket in a combination Lottery for the highest prize."[68] Although Henry's health was now robust, he admitted that Elizabeth did not enjoy good health and doubted that she ever would. "It is a great affliction to her & to me, but must be borne with patience."[69]

Throughout his life the personality of Henry Eno evoked comment from both family and friends. One Iowa associate thought him retiring and rather austere in manner, but even so he was always a favorite among those who knew him best.[70] Another Iowan described him as "highly learned in general literature and reasonably well versed in law" but then with penetrating observation went on to write, "he seemed to dislike its practice and labors, and would quit a law book at any moment to examine a specimen of geology or to go into a garden to examine and enjoy the color and fragrance of a new-blown-rose."[71]

68. Henry Eno to William Eno, November 22, 1846.
69. Ibid.
70. Taylor, *Annals of Iowa,* 1st ser. 10 (January 1872), 26.
71. *History of Lee County,* p. 543.

Early in 1844 Edward Eno announced his intention of also becoming a "western man."[1] Temporarily leaving his family behind in their former home at Kinderhook, he moved west to Island Grove, Sangamon County, Illinois, where he and a partner located on a 320-acre farm, expecting to raise sheep. While his brother Henry was practicing law and engaging in real estate speculations in the Iowa towns on the west bank of the Mississippi River, Edward concentrated on land and agricultural promotions in adjoining Illinois. His activities between 1844 and 1850, as revealed in the family correspondence, were doubtless typical of many pioneering farmers in this region. Like most rural dwellers in the prairie states, he hoped to gain wealth from the increment on land. A railroad from Springfield to the Illinois River passed along the southern edge of his acreage,[2] which was located midway between the towns of Jacksonville and Springfield. An attempt at sheep raising proved a financial failure, and he found he had leased more acreage than he could profitably use, as anticipated profits did not materialize.[3] On one occasion, unable to make the lease payments, he franticly requested financial aid from his father and brother William. Recognizing the seriousness of his plight, William agreed to advance the necessary $1,000, add the sum to the amount already owed him, and take a mortgage on the Illinois farm.[4]

Scarcely had this business crisis passed, when Edward reported that he was speculating in corn with a new partner.

1. Edward Eno to Stephen Eno, February 14, 1844. The Edward Eno correspondence in notes 1 through 7 is from the Yale collection.

2. Ibid., April 12, 1844.

3. Ibid., December 27, 1847.

4. Edward Eno to William Eno, January 21, January 22, February 9, 1850.

They were buying corn at prices ranging from twenty to twenty-five cents a bushel, expecting to sell it at between fifty and sixty cents in St. Louis. During the previous season corn had brought sixty cents, and the new crop in 1850 was known to be short in southern Illinois, Kentucky, Indiana, and Ohio. Edward had accumulated 15,000 bushels and shipped them to St. Louis. An incurable optimist and promoter, he also inquired if William's Pine Plains Bank would like to loan money in Illinois.[5] William did not respond to Edward's proposal and no doubt had reservations about his speculations in the grain market as well.

However, Edward and William were not completely preoccupied with business affairs. Edward had returned East to get Christina and their four children, and in writing home, after his return to Illinois, he always inquired of his father's health and urged William and his wife Eliza to come west to look at the country. He also reported on the education of his sons, Frank and Edward. "We have a very good school which the children attend, and are progressing rapidly. Frank has finished his Arithmetic and is now studying Algebra & Lattin. I hope to be able to give the boys a liberal education, that they may be intelligent farmers if nothing more."[6] Two years later he noted: "The boys have just commenced going to school again   The District have been building a new house cost $800. We have a graduate of Jacksonville College for Teachers & a very thorough man he is. It is to be known as Island Grove *High School*."[7]

Edward also confided in Henry about his family and business situation, and the latter wrote his father that Edward's "industry and enterprise deserve success. He may not make

5. Ibid., January 26, 1850.
6. Edward Eno to Stephen Eno, December 27, 1847.
7. Edward Eno to William Eno, December 7, 1849.

as much money as if he had remained in New York and
continued in business there—but I am satisfied that for one
of his constitution & temperament, (predisposed to pul-
monary complaints) he would not have lived long had he
not gone into other business . . . besides he has four very
promising children and if brought up within the corrupting
influences of such a Babel as New York is, the chances would
be much against them."[8]

Both Edward and William were concerned about their
brother Henry in Iowa. Edward had not seen him since early
1845 and finally complained in December 1847, "I have
not heard from brother Harry in a long time."

In December 1848 Henry broke the long silence when he
announced that he planned to go to California. He wrote
William: "You ask have the people in my country got the
California gold fever? I answer—Not as many as I would
naturally expect—but I have got the California fever and
whether it will turn out to be a California gold fever is to
be determined sometime hence—I have deliberately and
thoughtfully made up my mind to leave here the last of
February and find my way to San Francisco in California,
Elizabeth goes with me of course and is very willing to go—"

Gold had been discovered in California on January 24,
1848, when James W. Marshall, an employee of John A.
Sutter, the owner of a trading post in the Sacramento Valley
known as New Helvetia, noticed flecks of gold in the water
of a sawmill he was building on the south fork of the American River near Coloma. The first newspaper notice of the
discovery occurred on March 15, when a small announce-
ment appeared on the last page of the San Francisco *Cali-*

8. Henry Eno to Stephen Eno, March 26, 1848, Iowa.

fornian; ten days later a more detailed statement was printed in the *California Star*. Although news of the discovery spread quickly in California, the rush to the gold region did not get underway until May, four months after Marshall's find. The news first reached the Atlantic Coast in August, probably as a result of a story appearing in the *New York Herald*. Not until December 5, when President Polk reported to Congress that he had received official confirmation of the discovery from Colonel R. B. Mason, the military governor of California, did easterners begin to believe the reports and rumors.[1] Three weeks later the news had reached the Iowa frontier, and Eno had resolved to head for the Pacific Slope.

During the winter months, 1848–49, many men and women living as far away as New England and New York debated the advantages of migrating to California. Many resolved immediately to go just for the sake of adventure; others, who were in economic distress or dissatisfied with their lot in general, thought they saw an opportunity for a new start in life. Still others, uncertain of the economic opportunity offered, resolved that they simply could not afford not to go because of the potential opportunities in the new El Dorado. The Enos' situation was similar to that of many people. No pathway to success seemed opened to them in Iowa. Elizabeth was unwell and nothing seemed to help her; and the law profession was overcrowded. Henry reported, "lawyers swarm like the Locusts of Egypt—there is over 40 in this County & not one who makes a living by his profession." Fort Madison was in the doldrums, while Keokuk, twenty-six miles south, had become all the rage

1. The literature on the gold rush is extensive. Perhaps the two most valuable books are those by Rodman W. Paul, *California Gold* (Cambridge, Harvard University Press, 1947) and John W. Caughey, *Gold Is the Cornerstone* (Berkeley, University of California Press, 1949).

and was building up very rapidly. Crops had never been better in Iowa than in 1848, but prices for wheat, corn, pork, and beef were very low. Henry admitted, "There is no business I like half as well as farming, but I am too poor to be a good farmer." As he reflected on the opportunities California afforded, Eno thought he might obtain a political office when the region was organized either as a territory or a state. His Whig friends had given him a letter of recommendation to General Taylor, then President, presenting his outstanding qualifications for a judgeship if California were designated a territory. He confided to relatives:

> I shall ask for the appointment, with however but little hopes of succeeding—It is doubtful however whether California will be organized as a territory this Winter —but I shall go to Washington City look around me & be governed by circumstances—I would take anything that would pay my expenses or even a part of it—Jones one of our U. S. Senators was Surveyor General of this State & Wisconsin—& he did not know more about surveying than I do of Egyptian Hierogliphics but he had friends at head quarters.[2]

If California should become a state, without going through territorial status, Henry hoped to arrive in time to have a hand in framing the constitution. He also knew that lawyers would be in great demand to assist claimants who were trying to get their Spanish-Mexican land grant titles confirmed. In Iowa politics Henry had always labored at a disadvantage

2. Henry wrote two long letters to his brother William about the proposed trip to California. One of these, dated December 28, 1848, in the collection of the State University of Iowa Library, has provided the essential information used here. A second letter, dated December 31, 1848, in the Western Americana Collection at Yale University, is printed in full.

because he was a Whig and the Democrats were in the majority. From this standpoint, his move to California was going from bad to worse, for the Democratic majority there was overwhelming in the 1850s. Eno's plans were obviously uncertain, and he expected to be governed by circumstances: "I may be the Lawyer I may be an office holder or I may be the merchant and if worse comes to worse I may be obliged to work for a living."

The migration to California in 1849 was known to be full of hardship and uncertainty, but the Enos had no fear of danger or adversity. Those participating in the westward trek were young for the most part, but Henry was prepared to defend his decision in spite of his years.

> I am fifty years old—this may be to others an objection but it is not to me—I am not as old as Columbus was, when he undertook a longer voyage—Success finally crowned his efforts—I am poor, and have not much prospect ahead—this is a reason for going not for staying—I have not passed thus far through life without listening to the warning voice of experience—I have had some severe lessons & trust I shall profit by them—I have lived twelve years in a frontier country & am therefore better calculated to go to a new Country than if I had always been the Inhabitant of an old State—I have health & a sound mind—I am as youthful in feeling as when I was thirty—I am hardy & capable of enduring more fatigue than most of [the] young men—

Like all the Forty-niners, the Enos considered whether they should travel to California by sea or land. Most of those commencing their journey on the East Coast went by sea, considering it to be the easiest way. The shortest water route, both in mileage and time, was to go by ship to the Isthmus of Panama, cross the land on muleback, and resume the sea voyage on the Pacific side. However, one risked the danger of disease on the crowded Isthmus, and passage on the Pacific was limited and uncertain. Although the trip around Cape Horn was geographically the longest route for sea travelers, it was the most certain and most comfortable. In contrast to the residents along the Atlantic Coast, Argonauts from the Mississippi Valley followed the well-established land routes opened by the fur traders, mountain men, and pioneer settlers. All known routes were used simultaneously in 1849; in fact, every river valley west of the Mississippi contained men and women headed West. At first Henry decided to take a steamboat from New York to Chagres at the Isthmus, from there overland to Panama, and on to San Francisco. He himself would have preferred the overland route because he knew that he could easily ride fifty miles a day on horseback, but Elizabeth's health was a primary factor, and he thought the sea voyage was her only chance for life and health. The final decision was to be determined by finances as the ocean voyage was far more expensive than the overland trip. Henry carefully explored his financial status with his brother William. Most of the 184 acres of Iowa land still controlled by the Enos were already recorded in William's name, but Henry was eager to hold at least 90 acres as a place to come back to. This meant William would need to take a mortgage for the remainder, all of which Henry insisted was appreciating in value. He asked William:

> Would you be willing to help me further?—You have already done all that a brother ought to do for another & more than ninety nine in a thousand would have

The Miner's Ten Commandments. Broadside printed in California in 1853. Collection of Western Americana, Beinecke Library, Yale University.

done—You have helped me in my darkest hour & have
had no return for it. . . . I am willing to sign any paper
you will draw up, to relinquish anything I may have
in expectancy—& I further give you the assurances
of a brother that your confidence if success ever crowns
my efforts will not be misplaced—Can you secure yourself so that ultimately you will not be the loser if I
never come back? To what amount if you can would
you be willing to help me? . . . I shall ever retain I
trust the same affectionate regard for you the same
brotherly love if you decline helping me at all—but
I shall most assuredly go if life & health are spared
me & if I give the last dime I have on earth to land me
in California.

Like pioneers everywhere, Eno was full of optimism and
philosophically defended his decision to head for California.

When I arrive there I shall be governed by circumstances, I can do any thing any one else can—I can
practice my profession or I can work & think it no
great hardship—I shall endeavor to deserve success
and shall not repine if I do not obtain it—I go with no
high wrought expectations, & therefore shall not be
very much depressed if I come back no richer than
when I went—I do not suppose that any of the above
arguments I have used will make you think my determination any other than wild & chimerical—I know
it will find no favor in the eyes of my father, I regret
this but cannot help it I do not wish you even to mention the subject to Father at all for I would not give
him an unnecessary pang, or help cast a cloud over the
last years of his life.

In the end, for financial or other reasons, Eno elected to travel overland to California. With the abandonment of plans for a sea voyage, all thoughts of going to Washington to seek a federal appointment were likewise forgotten.

Although no record of Henry's 1849 journey to California has survived, his brother Edward wrote to William in December of that year: "Have you heard from Harry   I have not since he left fort Larime—I fear he may be among the Mormons. I saw a man a few days since that had just returned; he passed fort Larime fifteen days before Harry. He had a hard time crossing the plains & thinks there must be much suffering with those behind. He described the work at the mines as very hard & none but Iron constitutions can Stand it. Among the samples of Gold which he brot home was one piece of *five ounces*. The sight of California Gold is tempting, but the toil & risk in most cases will about make the difference between obtaining it from the Sands of California or the Soil of Illinois."[3] Next month Edward wrote again, "I begin to feel very uneasy about brother Harry. Have you heard from him?"[4] Again he inquired of William, "Have you heard from Harry recently? September is my last."[5] William eventually replied, "I have not heard from Harry and I should think it strange but he was never punctual in writing and I yet think he is in California."[6]

Edward was right when he surmised that Henry was among the Mormons, and that like many of the Forty-niners who started from Iowa, he had journeyed by way of Salt

3. Edward Eno to William Eno, December 7, 1849. The Eno correspondence cited in notes 3 through 6 is in the Yale collection.
    4. Ibid., January 22, 1850.
    5. Ibid., January 28, 1850.
    6. William Eno to Edward Eno, February 9, 1850.

Lake and the southern route into the Los Angeles area. Although the vast majority of Argonauts traversed the Great Plains and traveled across the mountains via the California Trail and its various branches along the central route, those starting in the winter season often chose the Salt Lake–Los Angeles Trail rather than risk an encounter with heavy snow in the Sierra Nevada. In general, the route followed was that opened by Jedediah Smith in 1826: through southern Utah, along the tributaries of the Colorado River, across the Mojave Desert, and through Cajon Pass onto the Los Angeles plateau. Some of the parties headed southward along the Colorado River, realized that they were traveling farther and farther away from the gold fields, and in desperation took a short-cut to the west and met disaster in the region later known as Death Valley. Twenty years later Henry wrote of having been six months on the road to California and of having gone "to Los Angeles & from there 240 miles east to work a gold mine in the Desert." (Dale Morgan has noted that those who traveled the southern route to Los Angeles in the winter of 1849–50 referred to a celebrated mine in the desert between the Amargosa and Mojave rivers. At least one also wrote of men from Michigan and Iowa who decided to go back into the desert and work this mine.)[7] On June 17, 1851, Elizabeth wrote her brother, John H. Knapp, from Los Angeles that she and her husband had just returned from a trip into the desert to inspect their mining operation, which had turned out to be a disappointment. The work was to be abandoned; the Enos had lost all that they had invested, they did not like

7. Dale Morgan, *California Manuscripts: Being a Collection of Important, Unpublished and Unknown Original Historical Sources* (New York, Edward Eberstadt, 1961). The typescript is in the Western Americana Collection, Yale.

Los Angeles, and were undecided about what they should do. Knapp was confused because he had received a Sacramento paper stating that a Mr. Eno had been named postmaster in Los Angeles and at the same time he had had a letter from a former Fort Madison resident reporting that Elizabeth and Henry were in Santa Clara on July 13, 1851, and still undecided about the future. Young Knapp wrote the Enos that they had better return to Iowa next spring, no matter what their luck, and invited Henry to go into the lumber business with him.[8] Apparently, the Enos did abandon their desert adventure and worked their way northward overland in California, traversing the Salinas Valley to consider its agricultural possibilities, and then to Santa Clara and San Francisco.

For three seasons, while the Enos were in southern California, miners from the United States, Latin America, Europe, and Asia engaged in placer mining operations along the rivers flowing out of the Sierra Nevada into the Great Valley of California. Although two-thirds of the mining population came from the area comprising the United States prior to the Mexican War, California society was notedly heterogeneous. Each group—Mexicans, Welchmen, Cornishmen, Georgians—contributed technical knowledge from their past experience concerning the ways and means whereby simple mining tools—shovels and pans, rockers, cradles, and "long toms"—could be used to reclaim the gold. By midsummer of 1851, according to California's leading newspaper, the *Alta California,* the easily worked placers were losing "much of their attractiveness, even to newcomers to the land of gold," because of the decline in their

8. John H. Knapp to William Eno, September 14, 1851, Iowa.

yield.[9] In fact, this newspaper suggested, "the excitement relative to California gold is now over."[10]

By the time the Enos arrived in the gold country, three distinct areas of activity had become apparent. Recently diggings had been opened up at the head of the Sacramento Valley along the Trinity, Klamath, and Scott rivers. Although this northern district was the largest geographically, the returns there were the least rewarding: transportation problems were more difficult, the Indian danger greater, and the men who worked there seemed to have less ambition and imagination than the average Argonaut, so that technical innovations were at a minimum. Anglo-Americans concentrated generally in the central area north of the initial discovery at Coloma, including the Feather River mines. Water was abundant in this region, experimentation with various types of mining were continuous, and rewards were the greatest. To the south was the mother lode, and the heart of this mining section was in Calaveras, Tuolumne, Mariposa, and Stanislaus counties. The greatest problem here was the limited water supply, resulting in many "dry diggings." Mexicans who had extensive experience working in mining regions with limited water, and who were more patient and less avaricious, tended to congregate in these counties closest to their native land.

Each of these three mining areas obtained supplies from a trading center. In the north the small camp at Shasta City sprang up; the Feather River miners depended upon Marysville merchants for equipment and subsistence; Sacramento supplied the needs of the miners in the central district; and Stockton became the gateway to the southern mines. Camps,

9. San Francisco *Daily Alta California,* July 17, 1851.
10. Ibid., September 15, 1851.

some transitory and others permanent, developed in the mining regions wherever a significant mineral discovery was made. Like many adventurers in this society constantly in flux, Henry was drawn to the southern region embracing the foothills of the Sierra Nevada and by October 1851, had settled down with his wife Elizabeth in Mokelumne Hill.

Mokelumne Hill was situated on the south bank of the Mokelumne River, about 800 feet above its level, at a point where an ancient river channel was uncovered. Instead of being at the summit of a hill, as might be inferred from its name, the town was located in a flat with hills several hundred feet higher both east and west.[11] Captain Charles Weber of Stockton had found indications of gold all along the Mokelumne River in the spring of 1848, and later in the summer a party under James P. Martin profitably panned gold on the stream. In the early autumn Colonel Jonathan D. Stevenson led up the river approximately 100 of his men who had just been mustered out of service; they washed gold along the bars of the stream. At Big Bar one of Stevenson's soldiers found a nugget weighing twenty-five pounds while getting a drink from the river. This bar was located on the stream just below the future Mokelumne Hill. A visitor in November 1848 reported twenty men were engaged in mining at Big Bar, but Mokelumne Hill first became important in 1849 and 1850, chiefly because the only store and boarding tent for miles around were located there. Periodically rich nuggets were found, giving Mokelumne Hill an exaggerated reputation as one of the most

11. J. Ross Browne, *Resources of the Pacific Slope* (New York, D. Appleton, 1869), pp. 50–51. More detail is found in James J. Ayers, *Gold and Sunshine: Reminiscences of Early California* (Boston, Gorham Press, 1922), pp. 100 ff.

notorious placer mining centers in the southern mines.[12]
In 1851 Frenchmen unearthed the rich underground channel along the slopes of the hill, and a desperate struggle,
known as the "French War," ensued with the American
miners for control of the most valuable claims.[13]

Mokelumne Hill was the most active mining center in
the area incorporated into Calaveras County. This political
jurisdiction was first created in January 1850 and re-estab-
lished in April 1851, with Double Springs as the county
seat. At the time there was only one building in this town
that served as court house, saloon, store, and hotel. The
boundaries of the county extended from the Stanislaus River
on the south, to the Mokelumne on the north, and from the
summit of the Sierras on the east, to near the base of the
foothills on the west.[14] The usual struggle for possession of
the county seat ensued, in this case between Mokelumne
Hill and Jackson, with Mokelumne Hill the victor in 1852.
The new county seat was only a slight improvement over
its predecessor, according to contemporary observers. One
wrote early in 1852:

> This morning early we started down to Moquolumne
> Hill as we have never seen the place we wish to see
> it once. . . . Then opened to our view the Town of

12. Richard Coke Wood, *Calaveras, the Land of Skulls* (Sonora,
Calif. Mother Lode Press, 1955), pp. 27–28.

13. The literature on the "French War" is extensive. The Calaveras
Chronicle printed invaluable accounts of early mining activities in the
issues of October 18 and November 1, 1851. Events are summarized in
Browne, *Resources*. See also *A Memorial and Biographical History of the
Counties of Merced, Stanislaus, Calaveras, Tuolumne and Mariposa,
California* (Chicago, Lewis Publishing Co., 1892), p. 165; *Hutchings'
Illustrated California Magazine*, 3 (May 1859), 488–93; and *Historical
Bulletin of the Calaveras County Historical Society*, 1 (April 1953).

14. *Daily Alta California*, January 26, 1850, April 28, 1851.

> Moquolumne Hill   it is built on a low hill sur-
> rounded by higher hills & some lower ones. The one
> we crossed going into the Town was several hundred
> feet higher than the Town.
>
> The Town consists of several hundred houses & any
> quantity of tents scattered around   some of the
> houses are on substantial frames. There seemed to be
> a brisk business doing the Town being full of people.[15]

Shortly thereafter an observant Scotsman also wrote his
impressions of the mining camp:

> I reached the town of Moquelumne Hill, which is sit-
> uated on the very brink of the high overhanging river.
>
> It lies in a sort of semicircular amphitheatre of about
> a mile in diameter, surrounded by a chain of small
> eminences, in which gold was found in great quantities.
>
> The population was a mixture of equal proportions
> of French, Mexicans, and Americans with a few stray
> Chinamen, Chileans, and such like.
>
> The town itself, with the exception of two or three
> wooden stores and gambling saloons, was all of can-
> vass, and it was not difficult to tell what part of the
> population they belonged to, even had there not been
> crowds of lazy Mexicans vegetating about the doors.
> . . .
>
> I remained a few days at Moquelumne Hill in a holey
> old canvass hotel, which freely admitted both wind and

15. Charles L. Camp, *John Doble's Journal and Letters from the
Mines, 1851–1865* (Denver, Old West Publishing Co., 1963), pp. 61–
62.

water; but in this respect it was not much worse than its neighbors.[16]

As soon as the Enos arrived in town, they built a home of frame covered with canvas, which they advertised as a "Temperance House" where "good boarding, good lodging, and a quiet home could be found on Main Street." Henry formed a partnership with Edwin Gates and opened a law office in the Temperance House.[17] In December 1852 a week-long storm developed, alternating wind, rain, and snow that climaxed in the flooding of streams in Calaveras County. The rushing torrents carried away cattle and agricultural produce, some miners were drowned, and mining towns like Mokelumne Hill were isolated. There was not a pound of flour to be had on any terms, and only six head of cattle were left in the corrals. The residents were surviving on frijoles and flapjacks that cost fifty cents each. The Calaveras *Chronicle* commented: "Such wide-spread ruin and devastation has never before visited California. God grant that the catastrophes already known to us, may be the only fatal effects of this fearful storm."[18]

As in Iowa, Henry Eno was soon immersed in local politics. In 1852 he was elected county judge, even though he was known to be a Whig in a predominantly Democratic community. Calaveras County had long enjoyed the unenviable notoriety of having more than its share of rascals. Joaquin Murietta was reported to operate from headquarters there and the county was the scene of many of his most highly publicized barbarities. Apparently Eno worked dili-

16. J. D. Borthwick, *Three Years in California* (Edinburgh and London, D. Appleton, 1869), pp. 287–88, 302.

17. Calaveras *Chronicle,* November 8, December 13, 1851.

18. Quoted in the *Daily Alta California,* December 29, 1852.

gently to eliminate this segment of the population for one
newspaper reporter noted, "On the day I got here, there were
five horse thieves sentenced by Judge Eno to the State
prison, and others are in waiting. At this rate they must soon
get thinned off."[19]

Eno attended the Whig convention that convened in
Sacramento on July 6, 1853, to nominate candidates for
state office. As the delegates arrived, the *Sacramento Daily
Union,* generally recognized as politically independent and
the most influential newspaper in the state (with the possible exception of the *Alta California*), predicted that events
would "disprove the charge that the Whig party is dead, so
often iterated and re-iterated by the Democratic press in the
State." The editor launched a tirade against the administration of Governor John Bigler:

> In the hands of the dominant party, the State has been
> plunged in three years into almost hopeless bank-
> ruptcy. She is involved in a debt of nearly three million
> dollars, while she is without a single public building or
> public work, which can be pointed to as the considera-
> tion for which this enormous amount of money was
> expended. We have no public Academies or Univer-
> sities. No common school system. No public libraries.
> No railroads or canals. And under the rule of the
> present party in power the people can hardly hope for
> an improved condition in our state administration . . .
> The people have been fleeced to fill the pockets of
> indolent officials, or to furnish fat jobs for those brawl-
> ing hangers-on of party, who are too lazy to work, and
> who expect to live on their *claims* upon the Democratic
> Party. . . .

19. *Daily Alta California,* June 23, 1853.

Let the right kind of men be offered, and they [the people] are ready to unite with their fellow citizens to drive all speculators, money changers, and job contractors, out of the political temple of the State.

The necessity of a reform, a change of men and measures, in this State, is conceded very generally by men of all parties.[20]

William Waldo of Sacramento was nominated for governor on the first ballot, receiving 345 votes to 39 for P. B. Reading. When the time came to select a candidate for lieutenant-governor, Eno's name was among five or six others mentioned.[21] There were 378 delegates voting at this point in the proceedings and 190 votes were necessary to determine the choice. On the first ballot Eno obtained a majority over three other candidates, some reports claiming he received 196 votes and others reporting as high as 202.[22] The Sacramento newspaper informed its readers:

Judge Eno is pronounced by those who know him well, to be one of the best selections which could have been made in the State. His location is good and his talents and qualifications beyond question. Judge Eno was originally from the State of New York, moved from there to Iowa, where he stood so high in the estimation of his fellow citizens as to have been run in the Legislature as a Whig candidate for United States Senator. He emigrated from Iowa to California, and has held

20. *Sacramento Daily Union,* July 6, 1853.

21. Winfield J. Davis, *History of Political Conventions in California, 1849–1892* (Sacramento, Publications of the California State Library, 1893), pp. 26–29.

22. *Sacramento Daily Union,* July 8, 1853. *Daily Alta California,* July 9, 1853.

for some time the office of Judge of the County Court
in Calaveras county. Such is the estimate in which he
is held by the citizens of that county, that they elected
him by over three hundred majority in a county that is
largely Democratic. He is withal an able and effective
speaker, and will canvass the State.[23]

In San Francisco, the *Alta California* joined the crusade,
stating that the Whig convention had "manifested a greater
degree of discretion and patriotism than is usually found in
such bodies." The editor proclaimed:

> The tickets of the two parties are now fully before the
> country. It is the duty as well as the privilege of the
> people, who are to be affected by the result, to choose
> between them; not as between Whigs and Democrats,
> but as between representatives of and advocates of two
> systems of local State policy; between men who have
> been tried and found wanting, and men who are fresh
> from the gold fields and barley field meadows of the
> country, and who have at least no apparent reason for
> betraying the trust reposed in them. The struggle is
> not for party principles, but for the spoils of the
> Commonwealth on the one side and State Reform on
> the other. We shall oppose the one not because it *is,*
> but because it is *not* Democratic, and support the other
> not because it is Whig, but because it is for Reforma-
> tion.[24]

The *Sacramento Union* agreed that the Whig convention
"has been rarely equalled by any political body ever as-

23. July 9, 1853.
24. July 9, 1853.

sembled for political purposes."[25] Editorial followed editorial in the majority of the state's newspapers in support of Waldo and Eno.[26] On election eve the editor of the *Alta California* wrote with deep emotion:

> Our hopes and prayers are with the popular cause today. . . . It is for the citizens of San Francisco, this day, to determine if these abuses shall be perpetrated. . . . Let us then to the polls this morning. Let the day be given to the work of State Reform. Let us, if but sojourners here, do a good deed for those who are to come after us. . . . Let us strike a blow for our adopted homes, for California and Reform.[27]

Returns were slow to come in. For a day or two the *Union* thought Waldo had won. In 1851 Calaveras County, the Democratic stronghold, had given Bigler a majority of over 700, but Eno's popularity there had virtually wiped out that advantage, and there were indications that the county might be in the Whig column.[28] The Whig ticket ran better than expected, though not winning, in the valley and foothill counties, but in San Francisco, where the Democrats had conceded a 1,500 majority to their opponents and the Whigs claimed a 4,000 majority, the vote turned out to be so close that the Democratic margin elsewhere was not overcome.[29] The entire Democratic slate was elected. John Bigler received 38,090 to William Waldo's 37,454. Eno,

25. July 9, 1853.
26. In addition to those in the *Sacramento Daily Union* and the *Daily Alta California,* see the *San Francisco Daily Whig,* August 11, 1853.
27. September 7, 1853.
28. *Sacramento Daily Union,* September 9, 1853.
29. Ibid., September 10, 1853.

though strong in his home county, polled 32,968 to Samuel Purdy's 44,498 and ran behind the entire Whig ticket.[30] The *Union* bitterly protested the corruption in the city of San Francisco. The *Alta California* also complained: "The most extensively organized force of fraudulent voters that ever existed was brought to bear in the city, and beat down the popular will. . . . It is a sad commentary upon the public spirit and independence of California, that the people should elect a man as Governor who is known and admitted to be the most utterly corrupt and unscrupulous man in the State; but so it is."[31]

Eno did not take the election of 1853 so seriously, admitting to his brother William that he had conducted a lethargic campaign and under the circumstances had no right to expect to win. His energies were now concentrated instead on the greatest business venture of his entire career, the Mokelumne Canal Company. The dire necessity for water to wash the gravels at Mokelumne Hill had become apparent quite early; as one traveler explained the situation:

> The want of water was the great obstacle in the way of mining at Moquelumne Hill. As it stood so much higher than the surrounding country, there were no streams that could be introduced, and the only way of getting a constant supply was to bring the water from the Moquelumne River, which flowed past, three or four thousand feet below the diggins. In order to get the requisite elevation to raise the waters so far above their channel, it was found necessary to commence the canal some fifty or sixty miles up the river. The idea has been projected, but the execution of such a piece

30. Davis, *History,* pp. 26–29.
31. September 8, 1853.

of work required more capital than could be raised at the moment; but the diggings of Moquelumne Hill were known to be so rich, as was also the tract of country through which the canal would pass, that the speculation was considered sure to be successful; and a company was not long after formed for the purpose of carrying out the undertaking, which amply repaid those embarking in it, and opened up a vast extent of new field for mining operations, by supplying water in places that otherwise could only have been worked for two or three months of the year.[32]

As early as December 1851, a town meeting was called to consider the feasibility of building an aqueduct to convey a stream of water from one of the forks of the Mokelumne to the town;[33] shortly thereafter, the Mokelumne Canal Company was incorporated, with Eno as president. Most of the canals and flumes of 1850 and 1851 were small undertakings designed to carry water only a short distance and for use in a limited area. The Mokelumne Canal Company was among the three largest water canals in California, from the standpoint of both distance covered and the expenditure of money, being dug almost entirely by gangs of laborers equipped only with picks and shovels. Where a ravine or canyon had to be crossed, a wooden flume or aqueduct was often constructed. If a ridge interfered, it was tunneled through.[34] A miner recorded the beginning of the Moke-

32. Borthwick, *Three Years,* p. 300. In essence this analysis of affairs was correct but in detail full of exaggeration: the elevation of Mokelumne Hill above the river was measured in hundreds, not thousands, of feet; the canal was commenced only 18 miles away rather than 50 or 60; the sponsors of the enterprise lost money rather than making it.

33. Calaveras *Chronicle,* December 20, 1851.

34. Paul, *California Gold,* pp. 161–62. The other two large undertakings were the South Fork Canal, 16¼ miles long at a cost of $275,000

lumne Canal Company on October 31, 1852: "Started early
this morning and went down to the forks of the Mokelumne
     all the River companies had quit work as the water had
risen so they could do no more   in the River some China-
men were at work on the Bars   The Mokelumne Hill
Water Company that is taking the south fork in a flume to
the Hill have their flume built below the forks."[35] By June
1853 the water had reached Mokelumne Hill. One newspaper reporter wrote:

> The deep diggings in the vicinity of Mokelumne Hill
> have been celebrated among the richest in California.
> They have always been worked with great disad-
> vantage, however, owing to the lack of water, but now
> they will all be worked clean to bed rock. They have
> already commenced the sale of water, in a week or two
> they expect to receive a very large dividend for the
> stockholders. On the whole it is one of the most promis-
> ing ditches, both for the stockholders and the miners,
> that I have ever known of, and what is more, I under-
> stand that it is almost all owned by the people in the
> vicinity and those who know the resources of the
> country.
>
> I have examined personally a good part of the work
> and passed through a tunnel 300 feet in length, which
> has been cut through a hill, and the canal taken through
> it. It is not strange to me, after examining the country

---

in El Dorado County, and the Tuolumne Water Company, which spent
$200,000 in a vain attempt to bring water a distance of 20 miles to the
town of Columbia.

  35. Camp, *John Doble's Journal*, p. 121.

and the canal, that the people are in high spirits at the prospect of golden harvests.[36]

When first projected, the canal cost was estimated at $100,000; by its completion to Mokelumne Hill, $250,000 had been expended. The excessive cost of this canal, and many similar undertakings, was the result of the high prices that had to be paid for labor and supplies, the exceptional difficulty of overcoming natural obstacles to construction, and the result of the inexperience of the builders, the optimism of the promoters, and the necessity of sacrificing economy to speed in construction. This canal's construction caused a large influx of miners, more than could be accommodated, who expected to utilize the water in opening up new gravel washing operations. For every claim that paid $10 daily in 1853, there were forty that would not pay $3. The average wage was estimated at $1.50 to $2 a day. Hundreds of men who were industrious managed only to make expenses. Thus, in spite of the imagination, industry, and speed of the men who built this canal, the water was not produced when there was the greatest need for it. A visitor to Mokelumne Hill at this time noted that the town had passed its heyday, and there was more water available than could be used.

> The streets run in all directions horizontally, perpendicularly and circularly. The buildings, with few exceptions, are of a very inferior order indeed, being chiefly constructed of canvas. The population consists of a sprinkling of all nations. The Americans constitute probably one-fifth of them French and Chinese three-fifths and the remaining fifth is filled up with the balance of foreign medly, fleas, and rats. No fire of

36. *Daily Alta California,* June 23, 1853.

consequence has yet visited this place. The water works
are in splendid operation, and one would judge from
the height of the reservoir that sufficient momentum
could be had to throw the water nearly to the third
heaven.[37]

In January 1854 the company decided to extend the canal
on to Campo Seco and other nearby mining communities.
Before the project was finally completed, an estimated
$600,000 had been expended and the original stockholders,
including Eno, had lost most of their investment.[38]

Early on Sunday morning August 20, 1854, Mokelumne
Hill was destroyed by fire. The house in which the fire commenced was composed of canvas and was "filled with segars
and varieties." In an instant the whole building was in flames,
and the fire spread to a nearby restaurant and stable. The
entire town was aroused by the alarm bell. The hose company was quickly on the spot, but when the hoses were attached to the hydrants there was no water. Debate raged
over whether the water had been cut off at the reservoir or
the supply exhausted at some other point. Unable to obtain
water, the fire fighters began tearing down buildings in an
effort to save a section of the town. When the flames were
finally checked, the community was in ashes except for a fireproof stone house on Centre Street and a stone building on
Main Street. Losses were estimated at $500,000. The Enos'
Temperance House had been consumed along with everything else.[39]

Toward the end of 1854 Elizabeth and Henry moved to
Campo Seco, where he could oversee the last work on the

37. Ibid., November 5, 1853.
38. *Hutchings' Illustrated California Magazine*, 3 (May 1859), 488–
93.
39. *Daily Alta California*, August 24, 1854.

canal company, now known as the Mokelumne Hill and
Campo Seco Mining and Water Company. This camp had
been settled by Mexicans in 1849 and was always one of
the most cosmopolitan mining communities, containing according to official reports, a population of forty different
nationalities. Fire also destroyed this town, in 1854, but before then it had boasted of "three thousand inhabitants, with
a bank, three hotels, many saloons and a brewery." Campo
Seco was quickly rebuilt, and placer mining continued there
until the late 1850s.[40] In August 1855 at this isolated camp,
so late in life for Elizabeth and Henry, a daughter was born.
Henry wrote his brother William: "California is the land
of marvels—its a prolific Country as I suppose you have
heard—Well to come to the point at once with my news—
Mrs Eno was confined a week ago today and gave birth to a
daughter—a fine healthy well formed little one—with the
very best of lungs & keeps them well exercised . . . the young
one is called *Carrie* after John Knapps wife."[41]

Meanwhile, the father of the Eno boys had passed away
at almost 90. Henry, who had been designated executor of
the estate, deferred to William, writing, "I am satisfied with
any arrangement made by you and Edward." Edward went
back to Pine Plains to assist in settling affairs. Henry suggested that all indebtedness to William be taken from his
third of the estate. In reality, he was far less concerned about
money than the fact that he would not see his father again
"in the land of the living."

Events had moved rapidly in California in the six years
after the discovery of gold. From 1848 to 1851 the annual

40. Wood, *Calaveras,* p. 37. For an excellent sketch of Campo Seco
see *Gleason's Pictorial Drawing Room Companion,* 5 (December 24,
1853), 409.
41. Henry Eno to William Eno, August 11, 1855, Iowa.

increase in gold mined, chiefly by placer operations, was very great. By 1852 production reached an annual peak of more than $81,000,000, but the rate of gain had slowed down, indicating that the maximum amount to be reclaimed in any one year had been obtained. This was confirmed by a sharp decline in 1853, and, although there was a slight recovery the next year, in 1855 the output plunged into a permanent decline. Even so, gold production in the United States had multiplied seventy-three times during the six years following 1848; the United States had become one of the largest world producers, contributing 45 per cent of the total world output in the years 1851 to 1855. The discovery of gold had also led to one of the greatest folk migrations in world history; the population of California, just under 100,000 in 1849, reached 223,856 by 1852. The vast majority of those who migrated to California actually mined for gold only a brief time, if at all, but like Eno turned instead to providing goods and services for the vast throng that had assembled on the Pacific Slope. By the end of 1854 the period of initial excitement was over, and those who had not "struck it rich" began to doubt that they ever would. Most of the water-washing operations along the California streams that could be carried on by individual effort had been worked out. Capital was required for those developing a quartz claim or processing underground gravels, and many miners who were without funds were forced to work for others at a daily wage or find another type of employment.

Like many Californians, Eno felt the financial pinch of 1854–55, which climaxed in the failure of two great San Francisco houses, Page, Bacon and Company and Adams and Company. The exceptional prosperity in California that had begun in 1851 and lasted until the middle of 1853 had led to overspeculation. Men had anticipated that gold pro-

duction, imports, the value of real estate, and population
would go on increasing and had planned accordingly. The
decline in production frightened people in the mining communities; consumption decreased, economy was enforced,
prices for merchandise and land declined, and interest rates
fell in San Francisco, so that by 1854, many miners had returned to the eastern states, some had turned to farming in
the Great Valley, while others had crowded into the cities
and towns. Immigration by sea in 1854 was half what it had
been the previous year. The first banks in San Francisco,
largely in the hands of inexperienced men and unregulated
by the state, had flourished in the years of prosperity, but
when deflation set in, they collapsed, and their activities were
so intertwined with the economy throughout the mining
camps that the entire state of California felt the shock.[42]

Henry Eno had invested his inheritance in a canal company in Amador County; all that he had was tied up between this project and the company in Calaveras County.
Like many others, he had planned on increased mining operations and population that did not materialize. He had
$10,000 invested in the Mokelumne canal, stock of which
was worth twenty cents on the dollar in 1856, and his one-
third interest in the Amador canal had cost him $2,000. His
combined mining claims were evaluated at $2,000, and his
house and lot were worth $400. However, he had pledged
a portion of his canal stock to obtain cash, and he and his
former partner, Edwin Gates, had an outstanding obligation
of $15,000. Henry's continuing problem was a need for cash;
he had between $1,800 and $2,000 on loan to others that
he could not collect. Once again he somewhat gingerly

42. John S. Hittell, *A History of the City of San Francisco and
Incidentally of the State of California* (San Francisco, A. L. Bancroft,
1878), pp. 215-17.

wrote his brother William asking for a loan of $800 at 10 per cent interest to save his investments.[43] He did not get it and apparently resolved at this time never to ask again no matter what his circumstances.

Although material success proved elusive, Henry cheerfully wrote about the glories of the California climate, the growth of agriculture and a diversified economy, on state and national politics, and about the prospects for a Pacific Railroad. Commenting on the state fair of 1857, he noted:

> Our State Agricultural fair was a great one—there were at least fifteen thousand people attended—the exhibition of fruit was by far the best I ever saw—in apples pears peaches grapes figs Almonds & nectarines we can beat all creation—in vegitables we can show "some pumpkins" one of which weighed 264 lbs—and one beet which will beat any other ever raised weighing ninety three pounds—[44]

Henry wrote an agricultural address for the occasion which was printed as a separate by three California newspapers.

Eno was blessed with a philosophical outlook: "My lot is cast in California whether for good or evil I cannot say but whatever it is I must be content," he confided. Throughout his life he seemed plagued by misfortune, partially as a result of unfortunate luck but more often because of weaknesses in his own character, which he readily admitted, and flaws in temperament. He was usually a dreamer, yet at times he was a realist. Speaking of his canal project, he admitted, "if it is a failure I'll try again. *Nil desperandum.*" Again he wrote: "altho I literally fulfil the command 'not to lay up our

43. Henry Eno to William Eno, September 18, 1856. The Eno correspondence cited in notes 43 through 49 is from the Iowa collection.
44. Ibid., October 18, 1857.

treasures here on earth' I don't know but what I enjoy life as well as those who do—'Hope' the poet says 'springs eternal in the human breast' & hope is left us—"[45]

The Panic of 1855 directed the attention of Californians to the need for political reforms. Municipal governments, especially San Francisco's, were directed by unprincipled persons; elections were manipulated or bought; there were scandals in connection with public-works contracts; and the courts were corrupt. Politicians reaped profits because of the apathy of the businessmen and the public; the Democrats were in power and the southern or "chivalry" wing of that party dominated the distribution of the spoils. As a Whig, Eno had reservations about Democrats and a basic dislike of the "chiv" group within the party. When his business took him to San Francisco in 1856, he quite naturally aligned himself with the vigilantes, for the most part merchants and businessmen who had formerly resided in the northern states, as opposed to the "law and order group," made up, in large part, of office holders and professional men with southern backgrounds. Eno displayed far more emotion in this situation than usual, penning one of the most powerful statements in defense of the second San Francisco Vigilance Committee on record, because he had been visiting with James King of William only three quarters of an hour before King was shot down in the streets, an event that precipitated the reactivation of the vigilantes.

Henry Eno, returning to politics as a means of bolstering his declining financial position in the years of economic depression, announced his candidacy for judge of Mokelumne County in the fall of 1856:

> if the Election should come off this week I should be elected by a large majority altho I am an old line Whig

45. Ibid.

> & now a Fillmore man & the County is the banner
> County of Democracy—I have once acted as Judge of
> the County for two years & made the only good Judge
> they ever had (you see how modest I am) but there is
> no knowing what changes may take place between this
> & Election day—the bitter feeling of party may swal-
> low up all other considerations—[46]

The office was a profitable one, paying $4,000 a year, and
Henry admitted, "that is what I now look at principally."
If he was elected, he had hopes of higher office. Politicians
had intimated that if he should manage to carry Calaveras
County, he might be put forward by a political combination
of the American and Republican parties for the nomination
to the United States Senate from California. He observed:

> Now this is a consideration to be taken into view but
> does not weigh so much with me as the matter of
> dollars & cents—I am of that age when I should look
> for something to make the evening of life comfortable
> or should I be taken away to leave those who are near
> & dear to me beyound the reach of want—this is my
> ambition.[47]

As time drew near for the presidential election of 1856, he
shrewdly observed: "It is impossible to say how our State
is going   great changes have taken place within the past
two months—Fremont and Fillmore have been gaining
ground on Buchanan, still I think Buch will win in which
case any air castles I have built will be dashed to the ground
—Castle building however I dont go much on now days—

46. Ibid., September 18, 1856.
47. Ibid.

sober reality stares me too much in the face."[48] Eno had sized up the situation well; he wrote following the election: "In politics our State has gone Democratic with a vengeance —I dont know what my politics are and would be obliged to any one to let me know—I shall continue as usual to be on the side of the minority."[49] The Democratic landslide was so overwhelming that Henry's personal popularity did not keep him from being rejected by Calaveras County at the polls.

Although the mining camps of Calaveras County no longer enjoyed the feverish prosperity of the early 1850s, once the depression of the mid-decade was over, Mokelumne Hill, Campo Seco, and similar towns were more permanently built. One newspaper reporter commented in the spring of 1856:

> Mokelumne Hill has improved rapidly within the last six months, many new fire-proof buildings having been erected, and several more now under way. Large quarries of a kind of *lava stone* in the neighborhood, which is soft and easily worked, greatly favors builders, and is being used to a great extent here—making a neat and durable fire-proof building at much less expense than brick or limestone.[50]

Less than two years later Mokelumne Hill was described as one of the largest and busiest towns in the southern mines, with wide and long business streets lined with hotels, restaurants, and stores of all kinds in fireproof buildings. Saloons were decorated splendidly "in San Francisco style," and many

48. Ibid.
49. Ibid., October 18, 1857.
50. San Francisco *Daily Evening Bulletin,* May 14, 1856.

gentlemen of leisure conversed on the street corners.[51] But the Mokelumne Hill and Campo Seco Mining and Water Company did not experience the good fortune of others. In the spring of 1856 the miners decided that the company was charging too much for its water and went on strike for a period of two months during the height of the mining season. There were other problems in the fall months when the water level was low. One correspondent reported:

> At the time of my visit, the main ditch or flume by which this vicinity is supplied with water, furnished only sufficiently for a half dozen companies, and this apparently having been used previously higher up the line, was apparently about as thick as cream which milkmen usually supply their city customers. Of course, under such circumstances, the greater part of the miners were unable to obtain water under any terms, while those who use it labor under disadvantage. I was assured by the residents that I would find the appearance of things vastly different if I could only repeat my visit in the winter season when the flumes and ditches, all being full, the miners leave the river and lower part of the gulches to work the higher ground.[52]

The economic depression in California was but a local prelude to the larger national Panic of 1857. Henry grieved at news from Pine Plains about the bankruptcy of friends of bygone days. To his brother William he wrote, "I am very glad to learn that the financial whirlwind did not reach you," and then admitted that the time had now come for him to leave Campo Seco and find a spot to settle as he was in his sixtieth year.

51. Ibid., October 10, 1857.
52. Ibid.

The written record is silent on the next seven years of Henry's life. In September 1859, the business section of Campo Seco was reduced to ashes in less than thirty minutes by a raging conflagration.[53] We know that even though Henry may have moved away from Campo Seco, he stayed in Calaveras County to serve as a judge for a time in 1862 and to campaign unsuccessfully for the office in the election of 1865.[54]

As years passed without correspondence, Edward, in desperation, began writing California officials for information concerning the whereabouts of his brother. A letter of February 1865 reached the Sacramento County physician, who revealed that Henry had been in the hospital for some time. His wife Elizabeth and his "little Carrie" were dead, and in his sorrow he had turned again to alcohol for escape from his afflictions. The doctor reported that Henry had spoken of his two brothers, mentioned a longing to join either of them, but was determined not to be a dependant.

No one knows what happened to Elizabeth and Carrie. Had Elizabeth, frail of body, whose health had always been uncertain and whose mental state had caused her husband, in anxiety, to express his fear that she would end in imbecility, finally broken under the strain of disappointment and economic reverses? Or were she and her young daughter the victims of a fire, the recurrent danger in the mining camps, or of an outbreak of pestilence?

At this time Edward was working for the Claims Department of the Illinois State Sanitary Commission in Spring-

53. Wood, *Calaveras*, p. 37. Other sources state that the fire was in August rather than September. See *Las Calaveras*, Quarterly Bulletin of the Calaveras County Historical Society, 4 (January 1956).

54. Wood, p. 148. *Monitor Gazette*, April 8, 1865.

field.[55] This commission had originated in 1862 as a voluntary organization to raise funds and provide relief for Union soldiers in the field or in hospitals. Shortly thereafter the legislature recognized this activity by providing appropriations from the state treasury to pay agents selected from the volunteer workers.[56] Edward, who was in his late 50s during the Civil War years, had thus found his place in the Union cause.

Henry Eno, after his sojourn in the Sacramento hospital, accompanied R. M. Folger, the proprietor of the new *Alpine Chronicle,* to Markleeville, California, where he was to work as a newspaper editor. Between 1860 and 1863 prospectors from the Virginia City, Nevada, area had examined the nearby eastern slopes of the Sierra Nevada all the way to the summit and located virtually every claim later incorporated

55. Apparently Edward's speculations in real estate and agricultural produce had continued right up to the outbreak of the War. Each year in the spring he contracted to purchase thousands of bushels of corn at a fixed price to be delivered during the summer months, and then in the summer contracted for similar quantities of wheat to be delivered at the time of the autumn harvest. In his enthusiastic optimism Edward had overextended his operations and almost succumbed financially during the Panic of 1857. He candidly admitted having lost $30,000 in a single year. Thus, after fifteen years of farming and land and grain speculation, without ever attaining the wealth he so desperately sought, Edward finally settled for a salaried job with the Claims Department of the State Sanitary Commission in Springfield.

The details of Edward's real estate and grain speculations can be read in his correspondence deposited in the Chicago Historical Society. See, in particular, the letters of November 10 and 29, 1854, January 1, March 20 and 24, July 27, and October 16, 1855.

56. *Historical Encyclopedia of Illinois* (Chicago, 1901), p. 293. For additional information see "Report of E. I. Eno, Sanitary Agent in the Department of the Cumberland, December 1864," in *Second Annual Report of the Illinois State Sanitary Commission . . . January 1, 1864 to January 1, 1865* (Springfield, 1865), pp. 81–83.

within the boundaries of Alpine County. These claims containing silver-bearing lodes were concentrated in the Monitor and Silver Mountain districts, the latter containing the larger mining population. By far the best mines in this district were at the head of Scandinavian Canyon, just west of the town of Silver Mountain, including the I.X.L., Exchequer, Lady Franklin, and Pennsylvania. The principal mine in the Monitor District was the Tarshish; the supply town was known as Monitor. To the east of the Monitor District at a higher elevation was the Mogul District, where the Morning Star was the most important mine. To the west and north of these three main producing districts was the Mokelumne District where the Uncle Billy Rogers mine, lying astride the Kit Carson Pass Road, had been located as early as 1855. The mineralization here was well stained with copper. On the western boundary of this district there was a settlement known as Summit City, not far from the Silver Era mine. In all, fourteen mining districts were established in rapid succession.

To the north at a lower elevation was the important supply town of Markleeville, on the middle fork of the Carson River, with a population of 2,620 in 1864. Although mining activity provided the principal justification for these settlements, enterprising ranchers had settled in all the valleys lying between the mountain peaks of the Sierra and were growing grains and vegetables and building dairy herds. Another important activity was the lumber business; millions of feet of logs and thousands of cords of wood were being cut from the forests and floated down the Carson River to be transported to the Comstock mines.[1] In the years

---

1. Information on the early history of Alpine County is difficult to locate, and when found the evidence is often contradictory. A basic and reliable compilation is William M. Maule, *A Contribution to the*

of discovery, these silver mines were in Amador County, but in January 1864 a proposal was introduced in the California legislature to create a new county, Alpine, out of that portion of Amador beyond the summit on the eastern slope of the Sierra to the Nevada boundary. This was accomplished in March; and in August 1864 the voters located the county seat at Silver Mountain by the slim majority of forty votes, amidst cries of fraud at Monitor and Markleeville.[2]

Within three weeks after Eno's arrival in Markleeville, news of Abraham Lincoln's death was received; the "loyal Union men" assembled in the City Hall, elected Eno chairman of their meeting, drew up an oath renewing their allegiance to the United States, and invited all who would do so to sign.[3] The Union Party had a substantial majority in Alpine County, but from the very first election its members fell to quarreling about the spoils of office. Friction had developed within the party over the location of the county seat. At the first convention of the Union Party in 1864

Geographical and Economic History of the Carson, Walker, and Mono Basins (San Francisco, Forest Service, U.S. Department of Agriculture, 1938). Summaries that must be used with care are found in J. Ross Browne and James W. Taylor, *Reports upon the Mineral Resources of the United States, 1867* (Washington, 1867), pp. 170–73, and Rossiter W. Raymond, *Statistics of Mines and Mining in the States and Territories West of the Rocky Mountains, 1870,* House Executive Document 10, 42 Cong., 1 sess., 1871 (Washington, 1872), pp. 51–53. The most valuable details on the mines, mining districts, and towns are those provided by traveling correspondents of the more influential newspapers of the State of California, such as the Sacramento *Union* and the *Daily Alta California* of San Francisco. For example, see the *Sacramento Daily Union,* August 4, 13, 28, 1863, January 19, February 1, 1864; *Daily Alta California,* June 15, 1864, July 24, 1865.

2. *Sacramento Daily Union,* February 18, July 19, 1864. *Daily Alta California,* August 13, 1864.

3. *Monitor Gazette,* April 22, 1865.

there had been a ruckus when twenty-one delegates were admitted from Hermit Valley, a precinct that some claimed had one house and not over a dozen inhabitants. When the candidate nominated for county recorder came from Summit City instead of Monitor, the southern and central portions of the county allied against the northern, or Markleeville, group. The *Monitor Gazette* and *Silver Mountain Bulletin* united in an attack upon the Central Committee and *The Alpine Chronicle.* The upshot of all this was the establishment of two Union Party committees, one called the Central Committee and the other the Regular Committee. R. M. Folger, editor of the *Chronicle,* still in Markleeville, aided and abetted the Central Committee. The Regulars were led by W. O. Hayes who had edited the *Gazette* in Monitor, then had sold it and gone to Silver Mountain in April 1865 to resuscitate the *Bulletin.* A temporary truce was arranged at a Markleeville Convention in July 1865, when a new Central Committee was elected by merging the two groups. The Regulars had the majority and therefore elected Hayes chairman. The first action taken was to move the nominating convention from the town of Woodford in the north, to Monitor in the south. The convention was a fiasco.[4]

When the time came to nominate candidates for county office Eno's name was among six or seven submitted to the party convention in Monitor as a candidate for county judge. Although he led the slate on the first two ballots, when the third was cast a resident of Silver Mountain was nominated.[5] Later a group of bolters, suspecting fraud, nominated the president of the convention for the judgeship, and he was energetically supported by the new chairman of the county

4. *The Alpine Chronicle,* August 24, 1867.
5. *Monitor Gazette,* July 8, 1865.

central committee.[6] Residents of Markleeville were still dissatisfied with such convention procedures. The *Chronicle*
issued a call for a mass meeting, stating, "it is not contemplated to nominate a new ticket, but only to displace those
who secured the nomination by the use of money." Eno
was nominated to oppose both previously nominated men.
The editor of the *Monitor Gazette* inquired about the reason-
ing of Union men who acted like Copperheads:

> Now we were in the convention and saw a good deal of
> rushing around and button-holing done by all con-
> cerned, but could learn of no money changing until
> next day, when reports were rife that money to a larger
> amount than we believed to be in the county, passed
> into the hands of delegates from the pockets of those
> who aspired to positions wherein they might work for
> nothing and board themselves. The charge coming
> from one who offered, as we understand can be proved,
> $80 for one delegate's influence, looks very much like
> the "pot calling the kettle black."[7]

The ensuing campaign was bitter, with both groups of bolters accusing the first candidate nominated for judge of failure to support the entire Union ticket in the earlier 1864
election. When the votes were finally counted, Eno was
elected.[8]

Eno wrote for the Markleeville newspaper for about six
weeks, from May to July of 1865, but soon split with Folger,
realizing that the newspaper proprietor's sole interest in the

6. *The Alpine Chronicle,* November 17, 1866.
7. *Monitor Gazette,* July 15, 1865.
8. Ibid., October 7, 21, November 4, 1865.

publication was to facilitate his own return to Sacramento as a member of the state legislature. In the political imbroglio of 1865 Folger and Eno aligned themselves with opposing cliques. Folger was forced to stand aside and watch Eno use the columns of his newspaper to obtain political preferment while his own ambitions were thwarted. Eno's election as judge gave him an unanticipated income, and when Folger debated matters of compensation for his editorial services, Eno used the financial disagreement to justify the break that had become inevitable.

After Eno's election as judge, he moved to Silver Mountain and at the time of his installation into office seized the occasion to deliver a lengthy and formal address to the residents of the mining settlement nestled in the peaks of the Sierra. The new judge considered it necessary to "make some observations indicating the course I intend to pursue in my official capacity," particularly in view of the fact that the district attorney and the members of the Bar had united in advising him that there was no need to organize a Grand Jury. Eno expressed personal reservations about the position taken by the district attorney, a political opponent:

> The only reason that caused any hesitation with me was the defalcation of the Sheriff and his absconding from the county, and the importance of having the Grand Jury examine into the acts of the Board of Supervisors and the books and accounts of the different county officers, but having the fullest confidence that the District Attorney will do every thing that duty demands of him, and also that if it shall be found advisable, or necessary, a special Grand Jury can be summoned.

The judge reminded the lawyers present of the dignity of their calling and urged them to act with responsibility:

> the officers of the Court are expected to fulfill the requirements of the law prescribing their duties. They will be held to a strict account for all their acts and doings. The members of the Bar, whose sworn duty it is to discharge their duties to the best of their knowledge and ability, whose profession is a highly honorable one, are directly interested in upholding and sustaining it, not only as able expounders of the law but as observers of it; their arduous duties if ably, honestly and industriously performed, will reflect credit upon themselves and their calling. There is no profession which calls into requisition more talent, ability, more unrelenting industry and unflagging zeal than that of lawyer and advocate; the highest order of eloquence, the most profound learning, the deepest erudition, and let me add the most sterling integrity, honesty, and truthfulness are required.

Eno, in turn, promised to fulfill his duties with dignity and dispatch:

> It will be my object to mete out the law "as I understand it" to all alike, the poor as well as the rich, the weak as well as the powerful—*Fiat justitia, ruat coelum* should be the motto of every judge. Fidelity on the part of officers of the law, and promptness on the part of members of the Bar in preparing and bringing their causes to trial, is necessary at all times, but particularly so in the present financial condition of the county . . . We have abundant reason to expect in a short time, when our hardy miners have more fully developed the

immense mineral wealth which lies within our ever-
lasting hills, a great influx of population; the most
casual observer knows that all that is wanted to induce
it is capital and well directed industry; but capital will
not be brought and invested where the law does not
give it protection from the grasping hands of the law-
less. . . . For my part, I shall earnestly strive to make
this County Court respected, and to do so, shall take
measures to have all the orders it legally makes obeyed.
. . . I ardently desire, as Judge of Alpine, to receive the
countenance and approbation of all lovers of peace
and good order, and so to discharge my duties as to
obtain the disapprobation of all violators of the law,
and to make as far as lies in my power the climate of
this silver county an unsafe and unhealthy one for
them. My only aim shall be to do my duty, my whole
duty, and nothing but my duty. Strictly, sternly, and
impartially. Let it please or displease whom it may.[9]

The Alpine County court was not always conducted
with such dignity. One citizen, who had been arrested for
stealing a gold watch and chain and incarcerated by the
sheriff, tried to burn down the jail, broke up the furniture,
ripped off his clothing, and lay on the floor nude. When he
came to trial he pleaded guilty, trusting to the mercy of the
court. An exciting court scene followed:

Judge Eno, after the prisoner had addressed the Court
in a penitent manner, questioned him regarding his
past life, and gave him some good advice, remarking
that he would be lenient with him, although his conduct in jail did not warrant it. He was then sentenced

9. Ibid., February 10, 1866.

to three years imprisonment at hard labor in the State Prison. This sentence had hardly escaped Judge Eno's lips when Lawler spoke out in meeting thus: "G-d d--n your old heart; you ought to set there until I come out." The Judge leaned forward and asked the Clerk if he had formerly entered the judgment. Being informed that he had not, Judge Eno said: "Lawler, your conduct shows you to be possessed of a depraved heart, and unworthy of sympathy, and I will add four years to your sentence, and now sentence you to *seven* years imprisonment at hard labor in the Penitentiary." The prisoner was furious at this stage of the game, and again held forth: "G-d d--n you: you had better be dead when I come out again."[10]

The sheriff removed the prisoner from the courtroom, full of excited spectators, and as he did so the convicted man cursed the judge, the sheriff, and the community, threatening vengeance. The local newspaper editor observed: "Judge Eno, for acting promptly in this case, is entitled to the thanks of the community for ridding us of the presence of a dyed-in-the wool scoundrel."

Serving as county judge was not time consuming, and Eno spent his leisure hours exploring Alpine County, recording his observations in long letters to his brother William in New York, speculating in mining claims when possible, and dreaming of far away places. He supplemented his income by writing articles and delivering an occasional afternoon lecture. In March 1866 he spoke before a large audience in Silver Mountain on his favorite subject—the establishment of a Library and Mineralogical Cabinet for Alpine County—and took up a subscription for the project

10. *The Alpine Chronicle,* June 12, 1869.

at the close of his remarks. He later presented the same lecture in Mogul and elsewhere.[11] In February 1867 he gave "the first lecture of the season" before the Alpine Library Association in the county seat, on the subject of intemperance. The press covered the event by publishing a list of apothegms including the following:

> He that has energy enough in his composition to root out a vice, should plant a virtue instead. The strong soil that produces weeds will also produce wheat, if planted and cultivated.

> Men do more harm to themselves than the devil could possibly do for them.

> One hour in each day wasted on trifles or indolence is enough, rightly used, to make an ignorant man wise in ten years, and the money worse than wasted in liquor, in ten years is enough to make the poor man independent.

> The apples of Sodom are mistaken by the drunkard for the fruit of Paradise.[12]

As long as Eno remained in Alpine County, he continued lecturing on this subject. *The Alpine Miner* noted in April 1869: "A lecture, subject Temperance, will be delivered in Alpine Hall, Monitor, tomorrow evening by Judge Eno. Let all turn out."[13]

The judge was also a champion of the mining industry in the county and seized every opportunity to praise the potential of the mines and urge investment in them. On at

11. *Monitor Gazette,* March 31, 1866.
12. *The Alpine Miner,* February 2, 1867.
13. April 3, 1869.

least one occasion he prepared an article for *The Mining and Scientific Press* of San Francisco on "Mining in Silver Mountain." He wrote the editors:

> When miners see and read an article in your paper, either scientific or descriptive, they place reliance upon it . . . You seek to establish the reputation of your paper, and to give it a widely extended circulation by dealing with stern facts. You deserve, if you do not obtain, success. The miner who buys a pick to enable him to look into Mother Earth, should also buy and read your paper, which, if he did, would in several instances save him a hard blow.
>
> I will try and give you some facts relative to the progress of silver mining in Alpine county as a trifling compensation for the reading of your paper, which I borrow from a friend, being too poor to buy it.[14]

By the end of 1866 Alpine County silver mines had passed their peak of glory reached in 1863 and 1864. Eno expressed the situation so elegantly that the editor of *The Alpine Miner* could not refrain from printing selections:

> The hard times have decimated, or rather shifted our population, until the chest or chess is mostly winnowed out. Silver mining is slow of development. In a museum in England there is one of the oldest silver coins known, found I believe, in the Island of Cyprus. This coin has on one side of it the representation of a tortoise (the slowest of animals), as emblematical of slowness of development. As it was with silver mines, when the world was young, so is it now; there are but few ex-

14. *The Mining and Scientific Press, 13* (December 29, 1866), 402.

ceptions—the famed Comstock mine at Virginia City is one. The mines of Alpine county will only give up their riches to those entitled to them, and only as the legitimate reward of labor and toil—not merely spasmodic labor, but to labor that has become chronic.[15]

The editor neglected to reprint this further comment:

Some of our spasmodic miners have migrated to the frozen regions of the North. To Idaho, Montana, Lake Superior, and Russian-America; some to the sunny South. They can all well be spared; there are some few who remain, and are still to be seen traversing around billiard saloons and rum holes, too proud to work, afraid or too lazy to steal, and too poor to *secede* or get away; they hang around as sign boards for liquor sellers, waiting for something to turn up, but never turning up any thing themselves, except a glass of liquor; but the determined, resolute, nil desperandum, never say-die-men, remain and work away, night and day, with courage and faith as strong as ever. They believe they have grounds for faith and courage, and these are some of the grounds of the "faith that is within them."[16]

With his usual philosophical outlook, he proclaimed his faith in the future:

The hard times have operated, as medical men would say, as a prophylactic. It has shown that the true remedy

15. *The Alpine Miner,* January 12, 1867. The article in *The Mining and Scientific Press, 13* (December 29, 1866), was initialed "H. E.," and "from its style and expression, we conclude it was written by our venerable County Judge Hon. Henry Eno," observed the editor.

16. *The Mining and Scientific Press, 13* (December 29, 1866), 402.

for hard times is to work harder. There is no truer saying than that "God helps those who help themselves."
The people in Alpine county are fast finding it out.
They are all, for the time, it is true, troubled with a
scarcity of money; but the present indications are, that,
before long (say two years), many will be troubled
with a surplus. But "man is born to trouble," and the
best way is to meet it with a bold face. It is to be hoped
that when troubled with a surplus of the root of all
evil, man will bear it with Christian fortitude and
resignation.[17]

Recognizing the desperate financial plight of Alpine
County, the California legislature granted the county the
right to collect tolls from the lumbermen who were floating
chopped wood and logs down the Carson River. When the
tax collector attempted to collect the rates authorized by the
Board of Supervisors of Alpine County, the Carson River
Lumbering Company appealed to Eno for an injunction
restraining the tax collector from demanding tolls. The request was granted, and the district attorney and county tax
collector went immediately to Sacramento and obtained a
dissolution of the injunction from a district court. Eno continued to grant injunctions to the lumbermen, and just as
regularly they were dissolved.[18] Finally Eno asserted that
the statute of the California legislature was unconstitutional,
as it attempted to regulate interstate commerce between
California and Nevada, a power reserved exclusively to the
federal government.[19] The feuding continued and was particularly acute because the clique of politicians with whom

17. Ibid.
18. *The Alpine Chronicle,* October 19, 1867.
19. *The Alpine Miner,* July 28, 1866.

Eno had associated in the county had sponsored the bill in the legislature. In July 1867 Eno was still issuing injunctions. *The Alpine Chronicle* commented on one court action: "The decision is just and proper, and one that ought to have been made under the circumstances. Judge Eno in acting thus, has shown and exercised good judgment, that evinces a desire to protect the interests not only of the county, but its citizens at large. The decision is highly approved of in the community. The people want no money unless they are entitled to it."[20] The California Supreme Court finally upheld the decision that Eno had made,[21] but the state legislature in 1868 was trying to pass another bill that some Alpine citizens hoped would meet the constitutional objections of the court. The measure passed the assembly but not the senate. The *Chronicle* editor did not want the lumber industry taxed, so he supported the county judge all the way, even though usually unfriendly toward him. *The Alpine Miner* was dubbed "The Alpine Wood Chopper" for siding with the mining interests and county officials.[22]

Eno's salary as judge was $1,800 a year. Alpine County had been born in debt, and its liabilities mounted higher every year so that the treasurer was slow in paying salaries. He soon resorted to issuing warrants, and the holders were faced with the choice of holding them indefinitely until the county's revenues were sufficient to pay them at face value or taking as much as a 50 per cent discount to obtain cash. Citizens who were so unfortunate as to hold county warrants were urging that taxpayers should be able to fulfill their tax obligation to the county by purchasing these past-due

20. *The Alpine Chronicle*, July 6, 1867.

21. Ibid., November 2, 1867; *Sacramento Daily Union*, March 7, 1868.

22. *The Alpine Chronicle*, January 25, 1868.

warrants.[23] In this way it was hoped enough warrants could be sold to a sufficient number of taxpayers for their market value to go up. Eno finally decided to force the issue. He presented the county treasurer with one of his warrants for immediate cash payment, and, on the advice of the attorney general of California, the county treasurer refused. Through his lawyer, Eno presented another warrant for payment; and when this was refused, the treasurer was handed a writ of mandamus to appear before the District Court to justify his action. Judge Theron Reed decided against Eno and the case then went to the California Supreme Court.[24] There were those who thought:

> This is the first stab of the Hon. Judge at the life and prosperity of the county. It was well known by him that if he was entitled to his pay monthly in gold coin, that the District Attorney was, and that the two salaries

23. Ibid., November 10, 1866.

24. Theron Reed grew up in Illinois, near Springfield, and knew Abraham Lincoln well. He came to California in 1860 and in 1866 was appointed judge of the Sixteenth District Court, including Alpine, Inyo, Mono, and Kern counties. He was twice re-elected. The judge became known as "Shot-gun" Reed when he decided to take action to end the abuse and disputing between rival lawyers in his court. He entered the room one morning with a double-barreled shotgun on his arm, cocked both barrels, set it on the chair beside him, and remarked, "Gentlemen, there will be order in this court today." Through the years he handed down decisions that displeased the large land and water interests. When the new California constitution was adopted in 1879, changes were made in the boundaries of the judicial districts. As Judge Reed lived in Bakersfield, he ran for the Kern County District judgeship, and the large landowners campaigned hard and contributed money to bring about his defeat at the polls. His life came to a close in Yreka where he had a humble abode in an assay office. *The Alpine Chronicle,* October 27, 1866, October 12, 1867. *Yreka Journal,* March 24, 31, 1909. San Francisco *Call,* March 26, 1909. W. A. Chalfant, *The Story of Inyo* (published by the author, 1922), p. 207.

combined . . . would take from the Treasury of the County at least two thirds of all her available revenue, thus leaving a mere trifle to apply on the other warrants drawn by the General Fund.[25]

The California Court decided in favor of the county in the case of Judge Eno vs. County Treasurer Carlson, stating that the judge was to be paid as the other county officers, and went on to say: "There can be neither redress nor correction, under the system, except by refusal to accept judicial appointments, or resigning them when they have been accepted, or by an appeal to the people." The *Chronicle* editor added: "Here, in a nutshell, is good wholesome advice. If a man accepts an office, with a stated salary, and is dissatisfied with the pay, let him get out of it and make way for those who can appreciate it."[26] The newspaperman also admitted: "Had the county been defeated in this suit, Alpine would have been compelled to take the benefit of the National Bankruptcy Act."[27]

The political bickering among the petty politicians of the county, so evident in the 1864 and 1865 conventions and election, became acute as the time approached for the election in 1867. In January 1867 Hayes began baiting Folger by stating:

The editor of the Alpine Chronicle is piling up candidates for different offices in the gift of the people of this county, until they are as thick as flies around the shambles. Hold on, Folger, or you will have more candidates than voters, as the number now in the field

25. *The Alpine Chronicle,* October 19, 1867.
26. Ibid., November 2, 1867.
27. Ibid., October 26, 1867.

will require two or three conventions to satisfy the present demands, without naming the independent cusses.[28]

Hayes was invited to resign his chairmanship of the Central Committee, formed, like the Regular Committee, as a result of the friction within the Union Party in 1864 and 1865, but he refused to do so.[29] Instead, he printed a "personal item," noting:

Brother Folger, of the Chronicle, has gone below, to remain, 'tis said, until after the meeting of the Union State Convention. We are fearful that by this untimely absence his political interests may suffer and especially the reconstruction of these Central Committees. Delays are dangerous, brother.[30]

In May, Folger announced his decision to run for the state assembly subject to action by the Union Party convention.[31] The *Silver Mountain Bulletin* scoffed: "His chances are four-fold greater in catching the Asiatic cholera than of receiving the nomination of that body. Acting upon the old adage that 'misery loves company,' he had named us as a competitor for the same office, although in the opposition ranks. It's no go, Robert; we're not on it."[32] The Central Committee decided at this point to hold two county conventions, one in June to elect delegates to the state convention and the second in August to nominate county officers. Hayes commented: "From various sources, we hear the prophecy that long be-

28. *Silver Mountain Bulletin*, February 2, 1867.
29. Ibid., February 16, 1867.
30. Ibid., March 23, 1867.
31. *The Alpine Chronicle*, May 11, 1867.
32. *Silver Mountain Bulletin*, May 18, 1867.

fore August, every aspirant for official honors will be in the
field on his own hook, as the binding force of conventions
is played out in this county."[33] Folger strongly defended
the political party convention. When the Union Party assembled in Monitor on August 13, there was another bolt
by the Silver Mountain delegation because a Markleeville
man was nominated for district attorney. To restore unity,
Folger withdrew from the race for the assembly so that a
Silver Mountain resident could have the nomination.[34]
There were those who began to doubt that Alpine County
would go Union in the election, in spite of the clear majority,
because of the lack of harmony. The defeated editor of the
Chronicle remarked, "We fear they will all go down in the
dust together."[35] The editor of *The Alpine Miner,* who was
less emotionally involved, had a suggestion:

> We have been "buzzed" so much this week on political
> matters that, contrary to our usual custom, we have
> been led to reflect on party politics, and especially the
> want of reliability of the convention system as an ex-
> pression of the voice of the people. It is unnecessary
> to mention the fact that with trading, buying and sell-
> ing, and otherwise "putting up" a convention of dele-
> gates to nominate a party ticket, the system has become
> so rotten that it is falling of its own weight. The leaders
> of either wing of the party, after using every means in
> their power to win, and, failing, will turn against the
> organization they sought to control, even though it
> result in the election of the ticket of their common foe,
> the opposing party.[36]

33. Ibid.
34. *Sacramento Daily Union,* August 17, 1867.
35. *The Alpine Chronicle,* August 24, 1867.
36. August 17, 1867.

The best system, in this man's opinion, was nomination by the people in a party primary.

Henry Eno became so heavily embroiled in this hassle that his career as a public official was in jeopardy. In the midst of the campaign the following letter addressed to the editors of the *Chronicle* was published:

> Noticing the last few days a person holding the office of County Judge of Alpine county very busy in our streets and on the corners, in the stores, offices, and workshops, and barrooms, holding low and earnest conversation with the inmates taking men one side, etc. etc., it naturally occuring to my mind that the general election is close at hand, it has suggested itself to make the following inquiries through your columns, for the information of the public and legal voters of Alpine County: Is it proper for the person holding the office of County Judge, before whom contested cases are tried for county officers, to be engaged in the business of electioneering for said officers, and thereby prostituting the purity of the judicial ermine to partisan purposes. And if so, would said Judge be a suitable person to hear and determine cases? I also wish to further inquire if it is usual for said Judges to make threat that they will break up the business of the citizens of the county unless they do their bidding, if so, was that the intention of the framers of the Constitution when they separated the judicial from the general election.
>
>   Legal Voter.[37]

Just as predicted, the Union Party went down to defeat in

37. August 31, 1867.

INTRODUCTION

September 1867. Folger announced he was removing the *Chronicle* from Markleeville to the county seat at Silver Mountain.

In October the regular term of the county court was held and Judge Eno empaneled and charged the grand jury. Two weeks later he was stunned when the jury reported a full-scale investigation of his own conduct. He was accused of voting illegally in Bear Valley, not his official residence. The jury report called attention to the registration law passed in the California legislature in 1865–66 "thereby putting a stop to the heretofore disgraceful practice of individuals supposed to have political influence traversing the counties throughout the State for the purpose of electioneering—and at the end of the day depositing his ballot wherever he happened to be and so far as any one might know of having voted at every precinct visited."[38] The judge was also severely censured for his suit against the county to get his salary paid in gold, and only "the benefit of doubt" saved him from indictment for "willful misconduct in office" on this score. Moreover, he was accused of doing the county a disservice by shutting off the toll collections on the Carson River. The jurors concluded their report by saying:

> The most efficient manner in which the County Judge can serve his fellow citizens is by a tender of his resignation of such office, therefor we most respectfully request him to resign the office of county judge, that one, impartial and competent, may take his place and preside over the law matters of the county.[39]

38. The full Grand Jury Report was published in *The Alpine Miner* and *The Alpine Chronicle,* October 19, 1867.
39. Ibid.

The judge immediately published a card in the county newspapers:

> The undersigned respectfully but earnestly requests a suspension of opinion as to the allegations and charges made against him in that report. One story is good until another is told; hear what is said on the other side before you form a judgment; do not condemn me unheard. An engagement made several months ago will prevent me from making and placing before you my vindication for a few weeks. The proud consciousness that I can fully exculpate myself, and the assurances I have received from many who know me well of the belief that the foul charges made in that report are without foundation, will sustain me until I have time and opportunity to wipe out and efface the stigma attempted to be cast upon my reputation. To the electors of Alpine County I would say that, if that Report of *that* Grand Jury has impaired their confidence and integrity I pledge myself that, upon hearing my vindication, again to stand before them in as fair an attitude as when I received their suffrages for the office I hold. I further pledge myself that no one shall have cause to regret or to blush that he was a friend of or cast a vote for
>
>   Henry Eno
>   of Alpine County.[40]

Rather than suspending an opinion on the matter, Robert Folger at last had his opportunity to vent his spleen against his former newspaper associate:

40. *The Alpine Chronicle*, October 26, 1867. *The Alpine Miner*, October 26, November 2, 1867.

If he had lived up to his professions he would not be placed in the humiliating position of begging his fellow citizens, as Judge, not to condemn him unheard, but would have commanded the respect which his age and position justly demanded. We presume our citizens have no desire to pass judgment, certainly we have not, upon the charges brought against him by the Grand Jury. But for the peculiar relations formerly existing between the Judge and ourselves, and the fact that he has used this office as a stepping stone to a position of honor and profit, require the statement of a few facts concerning the past actions, outside the charges of the Grand Jury, of Judge Eno. A judge should think and hear, but outside the Court should abstain from forcing his peculiar, and often times vindictive, views of law matters upon the public. For the past year he has been preambulating the county denouncing all who did not acquiesce in his opinions—social and political charging (lip charges, contradictory and therefore self-refusing) the county officials with crimes that required the impannelling of a Grand Jury; he denounced the Grand Jurors for not making a more thorough investigation, and ferreting out the scoundrels, and after attempting in this undignified manner to forestall public opinion, a jury holds a session, night and day, for ten days and faithfully investigates county affairs, and exonerating those charged by the Judge, he dismisses them by saying "they will receive the thanks of those engaged in plundering the county." Is this justice? . . . Previous to the elections Judge Eno stated that he should not vote for Gorham for Governor, neither would he for the Union nominees for County Clerk or Treasurer. This was his privilege, and no one has the right to impugne

his motives, but he was not willing to concede the right
to others, on the contrary he, the pure, stalked from
one end of the county to the other electioneering for
his favorites, and charging, by name, a number of our
citizens with having sold themselves to the District
Attorney. In one instance we know it was a most
damnable slander and under the circumstances un-
generous and disgraceful. A man who openly, on his
mere belief, charges others with bribery, and threatens
to ruin their business is not fit to preside over a court
of justice.[41]

Eventually Eno delivered a long "Vindication" to the
editor of *The Alpine Miner,* who refused to print it because
the newspaper's compositor had quit and the editor had to
"depend solely upon our three little girls to 'set up' the
matter for the *Miner,* rendering it impossible for us to com-
ply with our desire to do strict justice to all."[42] The judge
was indignant but unable to bring any force to bear. Finally,
the editor decided on his own that he would publish a
further statement:

It pains us to learn that Judge Eno and his friends believe us in league with certain parties in this county
to injure him. We hereby disclaim all personal feeling
in the matter and state that when we allowed the
publication of the Grand Jury report in October we
were not aware of the *animus* thereof, and one week
later would not have given it publicity . . . We would
further state that we consider the grave charges contained in the report of said Grand Jury unfounded and

41. *The Alpine Chronicle,* October 26, 1867.
42. *The Alpine Miner,* October 14, 1867.

originating from petty spite. We make this statement of our own free will, after finding that our refusal to publish a long vindication is construed into a feeling against the Judge, which we again disclaim.[43]

Folger of the rival *Alpine Chronicle* suggested that the editorial was "as rich a specimen of crawfishing as we have seen lately." He insisted that no explanation need be given for publishing a public document of interest to the people of the county and advised "our contemporary" not to publish material without reading it. The judge had not approached the *Chronicle* about publishing his vindication, even though its columns were open to all. "Judge Eno don't like us, and uses naughty language," commented Folger, "but we can survive if he can."[44]

Fortunately, the grand jury's charges were in the form of a report, and no official bill of indictment was issued that would have necessitated legal disposition. In fact, the statement was so full of bitter vindictiveness that the thoughtful identified it with political partisanship, and its effectiveness wore off after the initial shock had subsided. Eno had built up a strong combination of political enemies, led by the district attorney and county treasurer with whom he had crossed swords, and the prosecuting attorney used the grand jury as a vehicle with which he hoped to destroy the judge. The matter was laid to rest publicly, but Eno's correspondence reveals that his personal pride took a blow from which he never recovered. Alpine County was no longer the land of enchantment and natural beauty; he schemed to find the ways and means to depart.

The future of Alpine County was to be determined by

43. Ibid.
44. *The Alpine Chronicle,* December 21, 1867.

mining developments rather than party politics. Excitement
prevailed in the county in April 1867 when a rich strike
was made at the Tarshish Mine in Monitor.[45] The *Chronicle*
commented: "It is conceded that the Tarshish mine at Monitor is the biggest thing in the mining line on this side of the
mountains—Nevada is no where."[46] Several tons of ore
were taken to the Ophir Mill in Washoe Valley for reduc-
tion, and the superintendent returned with a "mammoth
silver brick," reporting that the ore produced $400 worth of
silver a ton, "making it the richest mine on the Pacific coast,
if not the world."[47] Plans were under discussion by the
Schenectady Company, owners of the mine, to erect a mill.
Within the month news also came of a significant improvement in the ore at the I.X.L. at Silver Mountain. These ores
proved to be small pockets, the excitement quickly subsided,
and those who had hoped for a return of the boom conditions of the early 1860s were sorely disappointed. At the
year's close there was again talk of the inauguration of a
new era with the arrival of Lewis Chalmers, assayer and mine
manager, from London, England, to represent a syndicate
of British capitalists headed by The Right Honorable William Henry, Earl Poulett. These Englishmen had organized
the Imperial Silver Quarries Company, Ltd., capitalized at
£500,000, to purchase a series of properties in Alpine
County, including the Michigan Tunnel and the Sovereign
mine at Monitor.[48] The local press announced: "We . . .
hail the appearance of Mr. C., the first accredited agent of

45. *The Alpine Miner,* April 6, 20, 1867.
46. *The Alpine Chronicle,* April 13, 1867.
47. Ibid., May 4, 1867.
48. Papers of the Imperial Silver Quarries Company, Ltd., Companies
Registration Office, Bancroft Library Research Program for the Collection of Western Americana in Great Britain. *The Alpine Miner,* February 16, 1868.

London capital to come among us with a determination to
see for himself as the commencement of a new era in the
history of mining in Alpine."[49] The San Francisco *Times*
also noted developments:

> The London Imperial Silver Quarry Company have
> lately sent out a very competent agent, by the name of
> Chalmers, to examine certain locations and interests
> near Monitor. Monitor is a small place, just in its
> infancy, nourished in the cold arms of the Sierras, hid
> away in one of the rich gulches of the mountains, where
> already Eastern and English capitalists have sent their
> representatives. Like other places, Alpine County has
> its disadvantages. The early rush of the mad men who
> furiously crowded the little towns in the crazy struggle
> for "wealth in a month," in the beginning, is over. And
> cool heads, with patient hearts, are now working to
> develop the gold and silver that lies imbedded in the
> hills.[50]

Another representative of British capital soon appeared on
the scene, George T. Coulter of Baltimore and San Francisco. As a representative of his uncle, Robert McCalmont
of McCalmont Brothers, bankers and investors, he purchased
the Mt. Bullion Tunnel and several adjoining mining claims,
at the mouth of Monitor Creek.[51] In spite of the systematic
influx of British capital to purchase the major mines of Alpine County in the next four years, the industry remained
in the doldrums. The editor of *The Alpine Miner* confessed
disappointment with the record of 1868 during which year
only four mines were being worked and only one making

49. *The Alpine Miner*, December 28, 1867.
50. Quoted in *The Alpine Miner*, January 18, 1868.
51. *The Alpine Miner*, July 25, 1868.

regular shipments of ore.[52] Eno observed the arrival of outside capital, urged his brothers to invest, but his own dire poverty precluded his participation in any mining revival in Alpine. Restlessness overcame him, and he began to think of trying his luck in Arizona or taking a job as a newspaper correspondent in Japan. An unexpected development elsewhere provided Eno with an opportunity to leave Alpine County, at least temporarily.

Rich silver discoveries were unearthed on the crest of Treasure Hill in eastern Nevada late in 1867, and early the following spring there was a frantic rush to the area, the White Pine Mining District was organized, and eventually a new Nevada county was created by that name. The "White Pine fever" broke out all over the western mining kingdom; prospectors from California, Colorado, Idaho, and Montana, as well as the nearby Nevada camps, converged on the new El Dorado. An estimated 12,000 miners arrived in the district in 1868 and 1869; promoters in the newspapers predicted the population would surely reach 25,000, and maybe even 40,000.[53] Beginning in November 1868 the newspapers in Alpine County were full of items about White Pine.[54] Scarcely an issue was published without an article reprinted from the *Reveille* of Austin, Nevada,[55] the *Territorial Enterprise* of Virginia City,[56] or California's *Stockton Gazette*.[57] No one was as lavish in exaggeration and

52. January 2, 1869.
53. W. Turrentine Jackson, *Treasure Hill: Portrait of a Silver Mining Camp* (Tucson, University of Arizona Press, 1963).
54. See for example, *The Alpine Miner,* November 28, December 5, 1868, January 9, 23, March 27, August 31, 1869; *The Alpine Chronicle,* December 26, 1868, January 9, April 3, 10, June 5, 1869.
55. *The Alpine Chronicle,* November 14, 1868.
56. Ibid., November 20, 1868.
57. *The Alpine Miner,* December 19, 1868.

praise of the new district as Albert S. Evans, editor of the
Alta California of San Francisco, who visited the major
claims—the Eberhardt and Hidden Treasure—and published a guidebook to White Pine.[58] Many thoughtless prospectors, reading these accounts, rushed to eastern Nevada in
the dead of winter, only to encounter extreme cold and
desolation and to wait four or five months before prospecting was possible. Eno had resolved to go early in 1869 but
was delayed until June because he had to wait for financial
assistance to arrive from the East. Even so, he risked his
judgeship by going, for the county supervisors were in a
position to declare the office vacant if he left the state for
longer than one month. The editor of *The Alpine Miner*
noted: "Judge Eno, who is now off on a flying trip, to San
Francisco and through Nevada, informed us that he intended
to be back in time to run again for County Judge and to
hold his October term of Court. The Judge is as full of life
and life's plans as a man of 30, and bids fair to outdo many
young men yet in his career of usefulness."[59] During the
summer months at White Pine, where he occupied a brush
lean-to along the slopes of Treasure Hill, Eno wrote highly
informative letters about the silver district and did some
prospecting, planning to return to Iowa or St. Louis if he
should strike it rich. The rush to White Pine turned out to
be one of the shortest and most intense in the history of the
West,[60] lasting only two seasons. In the end Eno, like most
men who did not arrive until 1869, realized that he had

58. Albert S. Evans, *White Pine: Its Geographical Location* [etc.]
(San Francisco, Alta California Printing House, 1869). See also *The
Alpine Chronicle,* March 20, 1869.

59. June 26, 1869.

60. Russell Richard Elliott, "The Early History of White Pine
County, Nevada, 1865–1871," *Pacific Northwest Quarterly,* 30 (April
1939), 145–68.

arrived too late to make his fortune, and he hastened back to Alpine County just in time to keep his judgeship from being declared vacant. *The Alpine Chronicle* recorded the Judge's return:

> On Monday evening last, Hon. Henry Eno, County Judge, arrived home from his visit to White Pine. Although White Pine is a rich mining district, the Judge believes that Alpine will ultimately be the true "poor man's paradise." Judge Eno reports that those who left this County last Fall during the hight of the "chloride fever" appear to be in good spirits, believing they have the world in the right place.[61]

The public did not know whether Eno planned to run for re-election.[62] His term as county judge expired in a matter of months, but he finally refused to run again, as the salary for the position had been reduced by the California legislature from $1,800 to $1,000 a year, not even a bare subsistence in a mining county. *The Alpine Miner,* in writing about the changed position, reported: "We learn it is the intention of the present worthy incumbent, Judge Eno, to leave the county within a few weeks."[63] The rival newspapers in the county even agreed as to who his successor should be; the editor of the *Miner* went so far as to suggest that the position of the county judge be abolished in the State of California.[64]

Henry Eno now announced his intention of returning to

61. September 25, 1869.

62. *The Alpine Miner,* September 25, 1869, stated, "We have not seen the judge but understand he will perhaps be a candidate for re-election."

63. March 13, 1869.

64. Ibid., October 9, 1869. *The Alpine Chronicle,* October 9, 1869.

the mining districts near the Mojave Desert, north and east of Los Angeles, where he had worked in the season of 1850. The Cerro Gordo mines in the southern part of the Inyo Range in the Lone Pine District had become active producers and had attracted the attention of miners throughout California to the southern mines. During 1865–66 the major claims there had been discovered by Mexican prospectors. Anglo-Americans took over the producing properties in 1869, erected two smelters in Cerro Gordo, and a third at nearby Owens Lake. The district was plagued by all sorts of problems: an inadequate water supply, refractory ore, and isolation. A regular freighting service was eventually established between Los Angeles and Cerro Gordo, along a toll road leading up Owens Valley, and stage lines were established to Lone Pine and to Aurora, Nevada. Scientific men and capitalists, both desperately needed, were turning their attention to the camp at Cerro Gordo with its 250 inhabitants.[65]

In November 1869 Henry Eno bade farewell to Alpine County, traveled by stage to Reno, from there by rail to Sacramento and San Francisco, and on to Los Angeles by sea. He observed the changes that had taken place in the City of the Angels since his last visit eighteen years before. Firmly resolved to explore a claim in which he had a fifth interest in the Death Valley region, he went forth in his seventy-second year seeking another White Pine or El Dorado. Between February and April of 1870 his prospecting trip, with guides and partners, riding on horseback and accompanied by pack mules, took him to Tehachapi, to the El

65. Raymond, *Statistics,* pp. 17–27. *Report of the California State Mineralogist, 1915–1916, 15* (Sacramento, 1919), 87–88. Chalfant, *Story of Inyo,* pp. 248–56. Chalfant, "Cerro Gordo," *Quarterly of the Historical Society of Southern California, 22* (June 1940), 55–61.

Paso mines in the mountains to the north of Randsburg, on
to Lone Pine in Owens Valley, and to the mines of the
Panamint Range along the western edge of Death Valley.
He had plans to take out five tons of ore and have it processed in either San Francisco or Los Angeles, thinking to
sell his mining claim for $100,000 if the ore should run
$100 a ton. At this point he was closer to striking it rich
than at any time in his twenty-year quest on the Pacific
Slope. The first discoveries in the Panamints were not made
until three years later in 1873, and in March 1874 the rush
began. The District soon boasted a population of 1,500 and
a triweekly newspaper, the *Panamint News.* Some ore
samples produced silver worth several thousand dollars a
ton. As usual, capitalists came in and bought up the more
promising claims, in this case Senators John P. Jones and
William Stewart, and organized the Panamint Mining Company capitalized at $2,000,000. If Eno had found the rich
ore, perhaps he could have sold out to these wealthy men,
as others did, for as much as $350,000 a claim.[66] He re-
ported developments to his friends in Alpine County; the
editor of *The Alpine Miner* informed those interested:
"Judge Eno, formerly of this county, has been heard from.
It will be remembered that the judge started off last fall on
a prospecting trip through the country bordering the Colorado river, in Arizona, Nevada, and California, where years
ago, before silver ore attracted the attention of the prospector, he remembered having seen 'indications.' We are glad to
learn that he recently arrived in Los Angeles bringing with
him several hundred pounds of fine silver-bearing rock from
Death Valley, and reports favorably on the district."[67]

    66. Chalfant, *Story of Inyo,* pp. 257–65. Remi A. Nadeau, *City Mak-
ers* (Garden City, N.Y., Doubleday, 1948), pp. 159–73.
    67. May 7, 1870.

Eno not only survived the prospecting trip but also made his way back to San Francisco. Here he became seriously ill with dysentery and had his wallet stolen, containing the remaining Alpine County warrants and his various mining stocks. His old friend Judge E. D. Sawyer wrote his brothers that Eno was exhausted in mind and body and desperately needed pecuniary assistance to pay his debts and procure transportation back to St. Louis where Edward was now living with his children. When Henry recovered enough to write, he apologized for having asked the judge to reveal his poverty and distress and insisted he would not have asked for help had he been well. After four months of waiting the money was received, and Henry wrote to William: "The Prodigal son leaves this morning on twenty four hours preparation for New York on the Steamship Colorado via the Isthmus." He admitted his health was so poor that he could not make the overland journey, but to stay in California "was to die." At 73 he was still resolved to make his own way but frankly admitted that only God knew how.

The curtain is drawn on the final days of Henry Eno's life. He did rejoin his New York family and lived out his last years on Broad Valley Farm, owned by Walter Eno, William's second son. Henry lived to the age of 84.[68] Actually his life story was finished by the time he left the Pacific Slope, a poignant account of nonsuccess—the lot of most men of the nineteenth century. Like so many in that century, Eno was exuberant in his optimism, perhaps naïve and irresponsible, and buffeted about by the hard realities of economics and social pressures. One is constantly reminded of Mark Twain's character of the Colonel in *Huckleberry Finn*,

68. Huntting, *History*, p. 334.

who always had a grand scheme for acquiring wealth and fame, and of Charles Dickens' Mr. Micawber in *David Copperfield*, who was eternally hoping for something to turn up to improve his lot. In a way, the Eno story is a depressing chronicle, yet one cannot fail to admire the philosophical calm with which Henry accepted, and perhaps understood, the vicissitudes of life.

LETTERS

Fort Madison Dec 31. 1848

Wm Eno Esq.

    Dear Brother

        I wrote you a long desultory letter on the evening
of the day I recd yours, but notwithstanding its length have
thought of several matters which I wish to communicate
and which I omitted. You enquired how Edward was coming
on & I believe I did not answer your enquiry, at least as fully
as I ought. I have not seen him the last four years. In a
letter I recd from him a short time since he informed me
that his children were all doing very well, that his wife
was in very feeble health, & that the cares of his family
devolved principally upon Augusta.[1] I had a letter from
Augusta in which she says she goes to school every afternoon
to recite. In a letter I received from him last summer he expressed himself very well satisfied with his business & said
it was the first year that he had really done well. He raised
an 100 acres of wheat but lost 500 bushels by wet weather.
He has put in 100 acres this fall & says it looks very promising. I have written to him informing him of my determination of emigrating & some expect he will be here to see me
in the course of the week. Should he do so I will write to
you. Of course my thoughts are principally occupied by the
one subject i.e. my California expedition. The complaint
with which Elizabeth is aff[l]icted [affected?] with is one
which I much fear will in the course of a few years produce
inbecility of mind, if it does not in fact terminate in idiocy.
The idea is to me a horrible one & I am determined to do
all in my power to prevent it. The journey to New York

    1. Augusta was Edward Eno's only daughter and eldest child. She
was a favorite of her Uncle Henry.

done her a great deal of good for a time & I believe that the journey either by land or water to California will cure her. I yesterday had an offer to join a person with whom I am well acquainted in a *land journey*. The journey can be made in about *four months* & costs but little compared with a sea voyage. I send you a paper in which you will see *an article describing the route*. The journey by land may be as beneficial as a voyage by sea. Every spring there are invalids from all quarters of the country who make the journey for the value of health alone. If unable to make the voyage by sea I shall go by land. I believe I have already done wrong to ask you to help me—& I do not wish you to do so if you do not feel safe in so doing. Most of my friends indeed all of them say, that I should certainly go to Washington City & that the chances are greatly in my favor of obtaining a good appointment. I once made an application for office when *Martin Van Buren* was president & I then *thought it should be the last time*—but I am not quite as modest as I once was. I shall wait with much solicitude for your letter in answer to mine & be governed accordingly. I have written to an old acquaintance in New York for information as to the expence of the journey, but from what I have seen & heard I fear that I shall not be able to go it. From him I shall also probably learn *what it would be advisable to take on from New York, that could be sold to advantage* (if I can raise wind enough)—*in California.* I have no doubt an investment might be made which would be immensely profitable. Will you correspond with some of your friends upon this subject and procure if you can, information as to how and at what expense the voyage can be made & what can be taken there by one emigrating. I *believe I would be a good merchant or at least as good as half of those who engage in the business.* What action will be had by Congress on the subject is very uncertain whether it will still remain a military government, be organized as a Territory, or at once be admitted as a State is still a matter of doubt. I want to be there as soon as I can, & should I go by the way of New York I should like to take with me the Reports of the Supreme Court of the U.S., Whites Recapilation[2] in 2 Vols, Kent's commentaries[3] and a very few others. If there is to be a State Constitution framed I want a hand in it. If a Territorial Government I should like the office of Judge. If there is any gold there I want that & intend to have it (i.e., some of it) It will be to me a strange land but I shall not be among strangers altogether. There are already there very many who emigrated to Oregon, were dissatified & went on to California. Among them is one very clever fellow who owes me $150. Col Mason the acting Gov of California is an old acquaintance, he was stationed about 10 miles below this when I came to this Country and I acted as an agent of his for two or three years. He formerly owned considerable property here. You have doubtless seen his report, I read it for the first time last evening.[4] He is the last man in the

2. Eno's reference is to Joseph M. White, compiler, *A new collection of laws, charters, and local ordinances of the governments of Great Britain France and Spain, relating to the concessions of land in their respective colonies; together with the laws of Mexico and Texas on the same subject* (2 vols. Philadelphia, 1839).

3. A reference to James Kent, *Commentaries on American Law* (4 vols. New York, 1826–30). Kent was the first professor of law at Columbia College [University] in New York. The first volume of his classic work appeared in 1826, Vol. II in 1827, Vol. III in 1828, and Vol. IV in 1830. All the volumes were sold out by 1830 and a second edition was published in 1832, a third in 1836, a fourth in 1840, a fifth in 1844, and a sixth in 1848. Eno could have been in possession of any one of the six editions of this four-volume work that was considered the most useful summary of the law of the day.

4. Colonel Richard B. Mason's report was written from the Headquarters, Tenth Military Department, Monterey, California, August 17,

world who would be carried away by any thing visionary. In all probability I shall find on my arrival at least an hundred persons with whom I am acquainted, By the time I reach there whether I go by land or sea I shall be able to read Spanish, I can soon learn to talk it, The old Spanish claims & grants are always a fruitful source of litigation, we have a Spanish claim only 10 miles below us & they have been at law about it for years. California has been settled over 200 years & now coming into possession of the Yankees the old records will be overhauled. Whites Recapilation is the best work of the kind and contains the history of the old Spanish grants & the decisions of the Supreme Court upon very many of them.

I will present another matter for your consideration. Would you be willing to give me a title to the property [illegible word] so that if I chose I could dispose of it & take from me a [illegible word] for the amount I owe you? Would you be willing and feel yourself safe to take a title for the property I have here which will be unsold when your letter reaches me—say 90 acres and advance me some thing and how much? I should like to retain my town property if I could, for I believe in 10 years it will be worth two or three hundred dollars per acre. For the property I have now sold I can realize very little after paying my debts, & the *difficulty about selling real estate is, that to obtain any thing like a fair price it must be sold on credit*. I believe you are a better financier than I am and I hope you will work out the problem that has been troubling my head for a good while.

1848. It was published as "California Message and Correspondence," House Executive Document 17, 31 Cong., 1 sess., 1849–50, pp. 528–36. In the company of Lieutenant William T. Sherman, Mason had toured the diggings in late June and July 1848.

Pray dont write me a letter with a thousand good reasons for staying here—for go I must—& I don't like to look at the dark side. Misfortune is bad enough when it comes. I shall leave my place in the care of one of the most faithful & honest men in this or any other country and he will make such improvements as I wish & keep taxes paid up. I am afraid you will be almost glad when I am gone so as not to be troubled with any more long letters right off. But you need not flatter yourself, If I once reach there and have pen & paper you shall have a whole volumn inflicted upon you.

Yours affectionately,

Henry Eno

A little more than a year since myself & a few others obtained a charter for a Division of the Sons of Temperance,[5] on the 27th of this month a year ago thirteen of us met & organised a Division. We have now 123 members & another Division in town has nearly 60, I shall write to day to the Grand Secretary of the National Division asking to be appointed or rather authorised to organize Divisions in California. I see by a Report that there is one Division there now but do not see the name of any specially authorised to form Divisions.

5. The Sons of Temperance was founded on September 29, 1842, at Temperance Hall, New York City. Each town, city, or county could organize a subordinate division. There was a Grand Division in each state and delegates from these Grand Divisions met annually as the National Division. The *Daily Alta California* reported the organization of a San Francisco Division on October 27–28, 1850. There were three hundred members in the city at the time of celebration of the ninth anniversary of the organization in September 1851. Eno's letter suggests that the organization was active two years earlier than the newspaper reports.

Mokelumne Hill Oct 12 1852

Dear Brother

Yours of Sept 2 was received last evening. We are always pleased to hear from and still better pleased to learn that you & family are all well & Father is still in the land of the living and enjoying life as well as can be expected. I have not been very well for the last three weeks, having had an attack of the jaundice. Elizabeth is not at present in very good health but is getting better. We went to San Francisco about three weeks since and the change of air from the mountains to the lowlands is the probable cause. I hope soon to enjoy my usual robust health. You wish me when I next write to give you a description of how we live, what my practice is what Courts we have. We live in the village of Mokelumne Hill in a story & a half house, built of as frail materials as would possibly hold together with a Canvass roof instead of shingles our bed room has two planks in it for floor about 15 inches wide each, the balance ground floor—the two planks being a piece of extravagance. The bedstead I made myself. Since we have lived here we have kept a sort of boarding house. The words Temperance House *neatly* painted by myself are over the door[6]   We

6. Beginning with the issue of November 8, 1851, the Calaveras *Chronicle* ran the following advertisement:

Henry Eno   Edwin Gates

ENO AND GATES

Law Office at the Temperance House on Main Street.

The issue of December 13, 1851, printed:

TEMPERANCE HOUSE, where good boarding, good lodging, and a quiet home can be found, on Main Street, a short distance below the Union House.

HENRY ENO

Proprietors

EDWIN GATES

The Union House was on the corner of Main and Stockton Streets,

hire a Cook pay him a *$100* per month, hire our washing
done at $3.50 per doz. We have Sup fine flour costing only
twenty two dollars per hundred. Good Mexican Beef at 25
cents per pound, fresh pork at 50 cents. Potatoes at 10 cents
beets turnips cabbage tomatoes the same sometimes higher.
Price of board $12 per week. We have made a living at &
something more. We have apples pears &c when we are willing to give 25 cents a piece for them. In truth we live well
enough and dont complain. 2nd question as to law practice
at present. None at all   I came here a year ago, had not
a dime in the world borrowed of a North Carolina friend
$200 opened this house run in debt as much as I could, paid
a Dutchess County man five per cent per month Int for a
little money I borrowed of him. Went into practice. Some
lawyers have tried to put me down, and they went down
themselves. Had considerable practice, charged high prices
paid all my debts & was instrumental in organising a Company to bring the waters of the South fork of the Mokelumne River to this place, a Company was formed Capital
$100,000, they made me President, my duties were such
that I gave up the practice & hope to make something out
of it. I have got all I [am] worth in the world invested in it
& if it is a failure I'll try again.[7] *Nil desperandum.* I am now

---

Mokelumne Hill. Both of these advertisements appeared periodically
through February 1852.

7. Water for washing gravel was a problem at Mokelumne Hill as
it was in many other camps. The company to which Eno refers was the
Mokelumne Hill Canal Company, which brought water from the South
Fork of the Mokelumne River over eighteen miles away. A flume ran
the entire distance; at the start it was 40 inches wide and 22 inches high,
but for the last four miles it was 2 feet wide and 5 feet high to control
the flow of water. The grade from the South Fork of the Mokelumne
for the first fourteen miles was 15 feet to the mile and for the balance
of the way 6 feet to the mile. At the head of the canal the company had

before the people as a candidate for County Judge. And
judge I shall not be elected, for this is the banner County
of Democracy, and I am a *Whig*.[8] As to our Courts we have
a Supreme Court Circuit Courts County Courts the County
Court has appellate jurisdiction in civil cases—Justice Courts
jurisdiction $500. Our practice is based on that of New York,
that is we have all the worst features of your practice and
some bad ones of our own. I dont like my profession, never
did, and wont practice when I can do anything else as profitable, it comes in play however as a dernier resort. I am glad
Stewart is doing so well. I hear occasionally good reports of
him—& hope to see his name in the Reports. I also hope
Walt will make a good farmer & will cultivate his mind as
well as his fields. I wish Mary[9] would study Spanish instead
of French & I would write her a Spanish letter. And if she
would come out here introduce her to a Spanish Cavalier

---

a saw mill that turned out 15,000 feet of lumber a day, which were
floated down the canal and used in construction. A large reservoir was
constructed to supply the residents of Mokelumne Hill with water at
a cost of $100 a day. Plans called for an extension of the canal an
additional eighteen miles through the mining country to towns like
Campo Seco. Wood, *Calaveras,* p. 30; Calaveras *Chronicle,* December 20,
1851; *Daily Alta California,* June 23, 1853.

8. Eno underestimated his political appeal as he was elected County
Judge, even though a Whig, in Democratically controlled Calaveras
County.

9. Stewart, William Eno's oldest child, was given his mother's family name, but as a young adult he became known as William S. Eno. Like
his father he was trained in law but soon became an investment banker
and eventually moved to Philadelphia. The second child was Mary, an
only daughter, who married Captain Matthew Ellis. Walter, the second
son, became a farmer, married in 1861, and died in 1884. Henry was
continuously interested in his nieces and nephews but displayed an
obvious preference for the girls by regularly commenting on the education and accomplishments of both Edward's Augusta and William's
Mary.

who owns as much land as would make a County in New
York. I am sorry to learn that Edward is embarrassed, he
deserves a better fortune, I wish he would come out here
wife children & all. If I go back next year which is doubtful
I intend to persuade him to do so—here is the place for him
& his boys. You say you some think of coming out. Now I
dont believe you will, and would not like the Country if you
did. The change from the sober monotonous life of Dutchess
Co to the go ahead bustling restless life of California would
be greater than even that of Climate. You say you have had
an un[us]ually dry summer. We had a rather wet one. We
had rain enough to lay the dust once since the 20th of April,
a thing very unusuall. The rainy season will probably commence between the first & 20th of December then all will
be green. The Winter is our spring, the summer our winter
of vegitation. Hay is worth with you $20 per ton. I have
bought for our Company 65 tons at $80. & $100 per ton.
I am now trying to sell my house & intend if I do so to build
another one a sort of 7 by nine hut, and live easier. Give
my love to Father & to all the family, Elizabeth would be
glad to receive a letter from Eliza   she sends her love
to all.

yours truly

Henry Eno

Wm Eno

Wm Eno   Mokelumne Hill Oct 28 1853
          Dear Brother
          Have just recd your letter of Sept. 14, had not
heard from you before in a long time. We are enjoying good
health & also enjoying life as well as any persons can well
do in our circumstances with plenty of work to do & always

boyed up with hope. I am glad to learn that you are all well
and all doing well—I hope Mary learns French, reads History Biography Geography, can make good bread & a good
pudding & will find time to write her Uncle Harry a letter
at least once every two months. I am still President of the
Canal Co. My time of office as Judge of the County will
expire the first of April—I was nominated by the Whigs
for Lieut Gov—but was not elected, ought not to have been
—so that matter is settled. A person in these days who would
take no more pains than I did to secure an election must
expect to lose. I expended $150 in travelling in some of the
Northern Counties and that is the sum total of what it cost
me. I dont regret it however I made a good many acquaintances & became somewhat favorably known. A few months
will determine the question as to whether I make any thing
from the Canal. I have all I am worth invested. I therefore
must make or break. If I succeed according to my hopes I
shall pay the East a visit next year. If not of course stay here,
or if the Sandwich Islands¹⁰ are annexed go a little farther
west. The best country you know is always west of where
we are. I hope Government will annex these Islands & as I
think, the sooner the better. I should like right well to have

10. The acquisition of California and Oregon had emphasized the
importance of the Sandwich Islands, or Hawaii, to the United States.
When France temporarily seized Honolulu in 1849, the United States
announced that she could not allow the islands to pass under the ex-
clusive control of any other power, but that this nation did not covet
sovereignty. In 1851 the King of the islands, alarmed at French aggres-
sion, tried to cede his domains to the United States. Daniel Webster,
as Secretary of State, rejected the offer and, consistent with Whig
policy, insisted that the United States favored the independence of
Hawaii but could never allow the islands to fall into the possession of
a European power. President Millard Fillmore appeared interested in
negotiating a tripartite self-denial ordinance with England and France,
but the election of 1852 transferred policy making from the Whigs to

it done, would turn Democrat of the young America stripe[11] for the sake of a good position there. If it is done, intend to have a finger in the pie. White who tried to kill me was sent to the penitentiary for two years. He will not come near me, when his time is out. About three weeks since business called me to San Francisco. Elizabeth went with me. I passed about a week at Santa Clara among some old friends very pleasant-ly. The past season has been a very productive one. We now raise a good deal of wheat, and the best potatoes & other vegitables in the world, it is not unusual to raise 50 to 75 bushels of wheat to the acre, and over fifteen flour mills are already erected in different places. I hope we shall not have to give a dollar per pound for flour very soon again. We have had no rain but just to lay the dust once or twice for the last six months. Expect soon the rainy season. Our town is now supplied with water carried through our streets in

---

the Democrats. Apparently Eno, as a Whig, did not approve of his party's policy but was for immediate annexation. Samuel F. Bemis, *A Short History of American Foreign Policy and Diplomacy* (New York, Henry Holt, 1959), pp. 181–83; see also Bemis, *The American Secretaries of State and their Diplomacy*, 6 (New York, Alfred A. Knopf, 1928).

11. The Young America Movement, largely within the Democratic Party, was devoted to encouraging the ideals of service and duty and to enlisting aid within the United States for democratic movements beyond the seas. Merle Curti has suggested that its "glorious ideals were as vague as they were grand." All those who participated had an exag-gerated, immature faith in the glory of American institutitons. Some wanted to spread these institutions abroad; others were interested in foreign trade expansion; still others wished to encourage democracy in Europe, but had no specific plan. Such a program attracted both idealists and materialists. The immediate impact of the movement was to create alarm in Europe; its greatest significance was as an expression of a new national self-consciousness. M. E. Curti, "Young America," *American Historical Review, 32* (1926), 34–55. The implications of the movement in foreign policy can be read in Thomas A. Bailey, *A Diplomatic History of the American People* (New York, Appleton-Century-Crofts, 1958).

Iron pipes which comes from the South fork of the Mokelumne River distant nineteen miles. And now while I am
writing the water is just brought to our door, I feel some
pride in it. A work of which I was the principal projector,
I have so far come through successfully. This will be handed
to you very probably by Chas. B Vail of Dutchess Co and
a particular friend of mine, he was one of the Trustees of
our Canal. Has been also employed as an Architect. He built
one of our Aqueducts of about 1200 feet long & 75 feet
high. He has just completed a large bridge across the Mokelumne River. He can tell you every thing in relation to our
works & this section of the Mining Country, but has never
travelled in our vallies. He is a noble hearted man an excellent architect & has been a successful miner. He returns to
stay he says—but I dont believe it, I expect him *back again*
in a year. Should he not deliver this himself I hope you will
take some opportunity of seeing him. You say something
about coming to California when the rail road is completed.
Better not wait so long. A rail road will be made & I think
two of them one North & one South. But it is not the work
of a day or a year. Gassing wont build it. The sun rises with
you three hours before it shines on us & it is a long distance
to overcome with even a railroad when built. To build it is
another thing, but it will be done. I recd a letter from
Edward he says, Augusta is East. He wants to come to California but cant at present. I really hope he will succeed in
some of his operations, he tries hard enough. Elizabeth sens
her love to all. I am glad to hear Father is so well & hope
to see him once more next year. But this is uncertain. Depending upon his health & my success in business. Remember me to all.

Yours truly
Henry Eno

Wm Eno Esq.   Mokelumne Hill Sept 12 1854

    Dear Brother

        Your letter of July 27 informing me of the illness
of our Father was received last week & yours of Aug 3rd
informing me of his death a few days after.

Altho I had reason to expect from his great age that
his life would not be spared many years yet I had fondly
hoped once more to have seen him in the land of the living
and I now regret that I did not leave here this spring & pay
him a visit. If I recollect aright he was born the 4th day of
Oct 1764, and would have been ninety years of age had he
lived to the 4th of next month. To very few is it given to
see as many years & it is very seldom that at that age the
mind of man has not given way. I would like to know the
particulars of his last illness & what physician attended
him.[12]

---

12. Stephen Eno died at his residence in the village of Pine Plains,
New York, on August 1, 1854, in his ninetieth year. A newspaper an-
nouncement pasted on the inside cover of his personal copy of the New
Testament commented:

> In early life he experienced many vicissitudes, and overcame diffi-
> culties that would have proved insurmountable to an ordinary man.
> From a humble beginning he passed on the full enjoyment of afflu-
> ence and position.

> As a lawyer, he was eminent, and for his knowledge, sought the
> foundation rather than the streams of jurisprudence; he had more
> regard for the principles than the cases, yet, was ever ready and
> intimate with the latter. There were but few, if any, who excelled
> him in clearness of perception and legal attainments. Probably no
> lawyer in the State has been more industrious, or continued for a
> greater length of time in the active duties of his profession, than
> Stephen Eno. Death only closed his course of reading and study. . . .

> He retained to the end in a most remarkable degree, the possession
> of his commanding faculties, and died as he had lived, respected by

I would also like to know what Rose[13] will do, where she will go and what her pecuniary situation is. The care she took of our Father for so many years, and her still remaining single interests me for her. I really hope she is well provided for & if not, will do all in my power to assist her, for I feel conscious she richly deserves it. My own health is very good but since the fire which burned down our town the 20th of last month Elizabeth has not been as well as common.[14] She is however about home. The Canal

---

all who knew him; having long since passed the "three score and ten" allotment and become the sole survivor of the men of his time, and the companions of his youth.

New Testament, Stephen Eno Papers, New York.

13. Rose was Henry's cousin and his father's housekeeper for many years. She became a part of the household in the early 1840s and Stephen paid her $1 a week, or $52 a year, in addition to her board and room, to manage his home. Eno kept a careful record of the daily expenses of the household. A dozen entries record his periodic payments to Rose. Among the last entries, that of April 18, 1853, stated: "Paid Rose Eno in full settlement for all past services $34.00." Stephen Eno Expense Book—General Household Account, 1814–December 18, 1825; Vol. II, Dec. 19, 1825–Jan. 29, 1852; Vol. III, Jan. 30, 1852–Jan., 1854. Stephen Eno Papers, New York.

14. A telegraphic dispatch sent from Stockton, California, on August 20, 1854, at 5 P.M. to the *Daily Alta California,* reported: "Destruction of Mokelumne Hill by Fire. A fire broke out at 3 o'clock this morning in the restaurant of John Ward, on Main St. The flames swept down Front Street, from Franklin to the ravine between the town, leaving only two buildings on Center between Lafayette Street to the bridge, leaving only Haskins' store and the Magnolia Hotel. The office of the *Chronicle,* with its contents, was consumed. No property was saved in the main part of town. Many Stockton merchants were losers by the calamity." The *Daily Alta California,* August 24, 1854, published more accurate and detailed information about the fire after the arrival of an extra edition of the Calaveras *Chronicle* furnished by Adams and Company.

is extended to a town called Campo Seco[15] twelve miles
from here and circumstances require my removing there.
I shall leave here some time this month and you may direct
your letters hereafter to Campo Seco, Calaveras Co. After
moving I shall work again. I wrote to Edward to day. Please
give my best respects to your family & to Rose. Elizabeth
sends her love to all.

Yours truly

Henry Eno

15. The miners at Campo Seco were reported to be doing very well
in October 1851. It was suggested, "The diggings will not last, however,
more than five or six months after the rains commence, as the area over
which they are spread is not very extensive." By March 1853 Campo
Seco was being described as "a very good mining camp." It was also
noted: "One might visit the camp and think there were but a few in
the vicinity, but on Sundays the place is crowded, showing a large population in the neighborhood." Calaveras *Chronicle,* October 18, 1851,
March 19, 1853.

In November 1853 a newspaper correspondent reported that Campo
Seco was situated nine miles southwest of the "Hill," and "from its
present appearance, promises to be a lively place in the event of water
being brought in. A canal is already under progression. The miners are
busily engaged in throwing up dirt, and fitting for winter." *Daily Alta
California,* November 5, 1853.

On January 23, 1854, the Mokelumne Hill Canal and Mining Company entered into a contract with John Andrews and Allen Cadwaller
to construct a canal to Campo Seco. The contract price was $95,000. Eno
reports that the canal was completed in September 1854; others place
the date a month later. Andrews and Cadwaller were given a contract
to build a reservoir about a mile northeast of Campo Seco for $5,000.
This resulted in litigation with the courts rendering a decision against
the company. As a result, a new company known as the Mokelumne
Hill and Campo Seco Mining and Water Company was organized. *Las
Calaveras,* Quarterly Bulletin of the Calaveras County Historical Society,
4 (January 1956). In December 1856 the Mokelumne Hill Canal Company was valued at $460,000. In October 1858 the Mokelumne Hill and
Campo Seco Mining and Water Company was appraised at $80,200.
Daily Alta California, December 16, 1856; October 20, 1858.

Tell Master Frank[16] I have bought him a first rate Indian Bow and Arrows & shall send them the first opportunity. Will always be glad to have letters from him & will write to him very soon

                                                           H. E.

W Eno   Mokelumne Hill Oct 20 1854
        Dear Brother
                I recd yours of the 11th of Sept on the 17th Sept containing a Copy of the Will of our father.[17] I also recd a letter from Edward last week written when at the Plains.

As regards the Settlement of the Estate I leave it altogether in your hands, and if you wish a deed from me of my interest send it in the form you desire & I will sign & forward it to you. Situated as I am I cannot of course act as an Executor neither should I wish to where [were] I a resident of the State of New York. I am satisfied with any arrangement made by you & Edward. It is now I believe eleven years since I was at the Plains and in that interval of time I have passed through so many exciting scenes have

16. Frank was William's youngest child and, like his father, a lawyer. He resided on the homestead and occupied the family law office in Pine Plains. His hobby was breeding fine Jersey cattle. He was also interested in the history of the Eno family and was responsible for preserving the records of both his father and grandfather.

17. Stephen Eno had made his will on July 21, 1827. His estate was to be divided equally among his four sons. Rufus was only 11 at this time, and Stephen designated Henry and William as jointly responsible for the "care and custody of his person & estate" until this youngest son was 21. Rufus died in 1845, nine years before his father. William and Henry were also named coexecutors; for this reason William had to obtain Henry's consent to make the final settlement of the estate. Last Will and Testament of Stephen Eno and probate documents, Stephen Eno Papers, New York.

experienced so many changes of good & evil fortune and the present has so called upon me for attention that the past has in some measure passed away from my mind. I however believe you hold an acknowledgement from me of my indebtedness but of what nature I cannot recollect nor in fact do I know the amount. Debtors have poor memories (exemplified in my case) however, whatever it is I want it paid. It is uncertain when I shall return if I ever do. I am now sorry I did not visit the States this spring but it would not do for us to pass a cold winter there having lived in this mild climate for five years. I should like much to spend next summer & fall in the States if my situation would permit it but that is very uncertain depending upon contingencies which may or may not happen. My health is very good, Elizabeth has not been as well as common, she overexerted herself at the great fire in this place the 20th of August. She is however about home. The probability is that we shall board out this fall & winter. The past season has been very healthy in California and the crops of wheat & other grain & vegitables very abundant. Flour is now cheaper in San Francisco than in New York. There is no better wheat country in the world than this State. One farmer harvested two hundred & ninety acres which averaged sixty bushels to the acre. And it is not uncommon to have a much greater yield. And we raise also as great a crop of rascals as can be turned out in Wall St. The Meiggs forgeries[18] are more than a

18. Henry Meiggs was a prominent citizen of San Francisco between 1850 and 1854. He was a lumber dealer and mill owner who became interested in real estate promotion in the North Beach area. Meiggs worked hard to expand the city in the direction of his property, and he expended large sums in development work. He was a popular man because of his ability, geniality, and tact, becoming known as "Honest Harry" Meiggs. He borrowed heavily, to finance his various promotions,

match for Schuyler financiering. The truth is both here & in New York stealing is considered shrewdness & swindling is only reckoned a fair business transaction.

I wish you would write me what Rose is doing or rather where she will now live & with whom and whether she has anything more that [than] what Father left her to depend upon. I am sorry to hear of Henry Welden's failure —he has been rich so long that it is hard to be poor. He is entitled to more sympathy than the poor Devil who has never been worth anything all his life. The railroad bubble has burst and thousands have gone with rail road speed to ruin. You are fortunate in not being caught on the tracks. Does Henry Weldens failure affect the Pine Plains bank? He was once mixed up with it someway, how, I dont know.

Elizabeth sends her love to all. Remember me to the family Rose and the few old acquaintances yet left at the Plains

Yours truly

Henry Eno

---

and when the price of real estate began to fall in 1854 he found his credit so overextended that he was destined for bankruptcy. At this point he decided to engage in a system of forgery by obtaining a book, or lot, of blank warrants on the City of San Francisco that had been signed in advance by the mayor and controller to minimize clerical work. He completed them as his need for money developed. This activity led to other forms of forgery. Realizing that his schemes had been discovered and his financial situation was desperate, he fled with his family to Chile. At least $750,000 had been taken. Meiggs later had a brilliant career as a railroad builder in South America. Hubert Howe Bancroft, *History of California*, 6 [*Works, 23*] (San Francisco, History Co., 1888–90), 765; John S. Hittell, *A History of the City of San Francisco*, pp. 218–26; Theodore H. Hittell, *History of California*, 3 (San Francisco, N. J. Stone, 1897), 434–41; Watt Stewart, *Henry Meiggs, Yankee Pizarro* (Durham, Duke University Press, 1946), pp. 7–17.

W Eno   Campo Seco Jany 12, 1855.

    Dear Brother

        I recd your letter with a deed enclosed & bill of
sale and have executed the papers and enclose them to
you.[19] You ask if all is right? I presume so and have no
reason to suppose otherwise. The amount due you was somewhat larger than I supposed but that is always the case with
Debtors if they let their indebtedness run on for several
years they must expect that like the snowball in rolling over
it will for [from] a small beginning make a large pile at
last. I have not your letter at hand. You however say I
believe that you can remit the amount at any time I wish.
I have come to the conclusion on reflection to have it sent
me, and should be glad if you can so arrange it as to have it
sent either by draft or bill of Exchange so that I can dispose
of it at San Francisco. Exchange or good drafts on New
York are worth at San Francisco two & half or three per cent
premium & I presume it would be no more trouble to you
to so arrange it. I much prefer to do any business I have,
through the house of Paige [Page] Bacon & Co at San
Francisco,[20] for I do not like the house of Adams &

19. When the estate was settled, Henry deeded to William his one-
third interest in the family homestead and lots owned by his father in
Pine Plains for $500 in cash. Indenture of January 9, 1855, between
Henry Eno of Campo Seco, California and William Eno of Pine Plains,
New York. Stephen Eno Papers, New York.

20. Page, Bacon and Company, a St. Louis bank, opened a branch
in San Francisco in 1850 that became a leading financial establishment
in the State. The St. Louis firm became involved in making loans to the
Ohio and Mississippi Railroad, running from Cincinnati to St. Louis,
and overextended its resources. A partner from St. Louis came to San
Francisco to obtain a million dollars worth of gold dust in an attempt
to save the Missouri firm from failure. He managed to depart before the
arrival of a ship with the news that the bank was insolvent. When the
news spread, there was a violent run on the San Francisco bank on

Co[21] because they have not treated me well. As I wrote you in my last letter I cannot now say how my business is situated every thing depending upon circumstances but I am striving to bring every thing to a a focus as soon as soon [sic] as possible. You express a wish that Elizabeth & I should pay you a visit this year if possible. We have expected to return but have experienced so many dissappointments that I now give up the idea altogether. My lot is cast in California whether for good or evil I cannot say but whatever it is I must be content. I had expected to have gone to San Francisco this week but as events have turned up it did not become necessary for me to do so & Elizabeth having an old friend there who sent her a pressing invitation to spend a few weeks with her she left yesterday & perhaps will stay until the fore part of Feby as my business will then call me to San Francisco. She has several acquaintances there who will make the visit a pleasant one. I was glad to have her go for I shall necessarily have to be absent a good deal for two or three weeks. I have

---

February 17, 1855. For several days the firm remained open paying out almost all the money it had. By February 23, 1855, most San Francisco banks had closed their doors. Bancroft, *History*, 7, 173 ff.; John S. Hittell, pp. 226, 229–30; Theodore H. Hittell, *3, 443–48.*

21. Adams and Company, expressmen of Boston, opened a branch house in San Francisco in 1849 and soon made larger shipments of gold to New York than any other house. A banking department was added to the firm. At first the company's express routes did not extend eastward beyond Sacramento and Stockton, but by 1853 they had fanned out into the mining communities and were without question the leading business house of the State, dealing with more people, handling more money, making more extensive loans for business expansion, and earning more profit than any other firm. When the crisis of February 1855 developed, Adams and Company closed its doors without waiting for a run. The money and bullion on hand became a prize for creditors and their lawyers to struggle over for seven years. In the end many depositors concluded that they had been deliberately defrauded. John S. Hittell, pp. 227–33; Theodore H. Hittell, *3, 442–53.*

a good deal of business at the next term of our District
Court which is held at Mokelumne Hill the first week of
Feby & immediately after Court shall leave for San Francisco. The last week we have had some rain the first that has
fallen of any consequences since last May. My health was
never better—& Elizabeth has enjoyed much better health
for the last three months than usual.

Give my love to all

Yours truly

Henry Eno

Wm Eno Esq   Campo Seco Jany 22 1855
    Dear Brother
            I wrote you about a week since & in my letter
stated that after reflection I had concluded to have you remit
the amount which would be coming to me & wished it sent in
such a manner as that I could sell the draft or bill of exchange at San Francisco. I also enclosed in the letter the
papers you sent duly executed & acknowledged. I write
this merely to inform you of what I had done in case of my
previous letter not reaching you. I should much like to receive the amount by the 15th of March if possible but if not
must do as well as I can. I believe I wrote you that Elizabeth
had gone to San Francisco to visit some old friends & that
she would probably stay until I went down which will be
about the 10th of Feby. I have received two letters from her.
She was well & enjoying her visit. I do not know that I have
any thing of interest to write about. I enjoy excellent
health   last Friday took an excursion on foot with some
young friends & between eight o'clock in the morning & five
in the afternoon travelled at least twenty four miles up &

down some pretty tall hills & felt none the worse of the exercise. We have delightful weather clear cloudless skies, & today has been like a summers day in June. But miners & farmers complain for the want of water   I have not heard from Edward for a good while   I am afraid he has been tempted by speculation until he got into deep water. I wish you would write about him.

Very truly

Yours Henry Eno

Calaveras Co

Wm Eno Esq   Campo Seco April 10 1855

    Dear Brother

       I recd yours of the 10th of Feby enclosing a draft for $1295 and shortly after receiving it had occasion to go to San Francisco and intended answering the letter but have neglected it longer than I should   I was absent about two weeks and on my return found yours of the 27th of Feby. I did not sell the draft at San Francisco and do not now know when I shall. Shall probably keep it a month or more. You have heard ere this will reach you of the crash of Adams & Co, of the suspension of Page Bacon & Co & Wells & Fargo. I went to San Francisco on some business connected with the house of Adams & Co. That house will never resume business here. They are hopelessly insolvent & their paper is selling at twenty five cents on the dollar. Adams claims to be a special partner here—but by our law he cannot be considered other than a general partner, and so liable for all demands here. I understand heavy demands have been sent east for collection, & many think that the failure of the House here will so seriously affect Adams that he must fail in the States. Page & Bacon have resumed business & so have Wells & Fargo, but many large houses have gone down and more must follow. The past winter has been remarkably dry, but little rain falling. We have had no cold weather—no snow & but little frost—flowers have been in bloom all winter. If California has no other in[du]cements but that of climate it would be sufficient to incline me to make it my residence for life. But I do not want to live here in the mines always. I should like to take up my residence at San Francisco or at some pleasant town on the coast. If fortune favors me I shall do so. Elizabeth is now enjoying very good health for her. My own health was never better. I rode yesterday on horseback between thirty five & forty miles and was no more fatigued. But I am getting old. I now use spectacles in the evening. Can get along without in the day. I am pleased to hear of Stewarts success in life. I have seen a number of persons from Dutchess who speak very well of him. Elizabeth sends her love to Eliza & the family. Remember me to all

Yours truly

Henry Eno

Wm Eno   Campo Seco Oct 3 1856
   Dear Brother
       Yours of Aug 15th was received last mail but not in time to answer it. I am glad always to have you write particularly about Stewart Mary Walter & Frank. I find by your letter that you have in a measure relinquished the profession which you have practiced so long & that Stewart is laboring at it. I hear good accounts of him & that he occupies a good position for a young man. I think you ex-

tremely fortunate in your children—from your no longer being solicitous about obtaining legal business I draw the inference that you are independent in your circumstances. Well I have been aiming at that myself but have proved a poor marksman but as my motto has been "nil desperandum" must pick my flint & try again. I've a little one to work for live for & shall never say *die*. We are well at present. I believe I wrote to Mary that Elizabeth had been very sick. She is now well. Little Carrie is well as ever, runs about everywhere begins to talk & is as full of mischief as a monkey. Wish you could see her. Think you would be proud of your niece. I was also glad to hear from old friends. Dr. W. Montevich[?]. Myers. Sam, Dick & Ed Hunting. Burnass[?] & B Culver[?]. I suppose they are all rich. But old time has as little respect for the rich as for the poor & I presume it has laid its heavy hand upon them as well as upon me. It has whitened my hair & somewhat dimmed my eye but still my feelings are as youthful as ever. I am sorry the Culver family are at war with each other about their father's property. It seems to me not only foolish but unnatural. Each had better yield something. They would think better of themselves should they do so. Others certainly would. Better kiss & make friends than fee lawyers & make enemies. I should like to hear of Zada who married Wm Smith. Also of Adam Strever & his children & I wish you to remember me to Rose & tell me how she is & with whom is she living. You ask me what is to be the result of the Vigilance Committee of San Francisco? Before this reaches you you will have seen by the papers that they have disbanded, but three taps of the Monumental bell would call them into existence again & crowd the streets with armed men in fifteen minutes. You are right in your conjectures that I upheld them. I was in San Francisco when James King of Wm was shot down in the streets. I had left him only three quarters of an hour before & it was only by accident that I did not stay & accompany him down street. He was a warm friend of mine & was truly a noble hearted man. He had bitter enemies, as all energetic active men have. I upheld the Vigilance committee because law was powerless to protect the innocent or punish the guilty, because the officers of law were corrupt, because the ballot box no longer expressed the will of voters, because men were in office who never were elected & because there was a combination of gamblers New York shoulder strickers and bowie knife Chivalry who ruled and whose only aim was to ruin. I believe the Vigilance Committee did right in hanging the men they did & banishing others & if they had gone farther & hung a Judge or two with the Sheriff and half a dozen of his deputies & about one hundred & fifteen or sixteen lawyers of San Francisco they would have done Gods service. The United States government had better never interfere with us by sending troops to put us down and help us to settle our little difficulties. They had better let us alone. It would not take much to set the people a thinking about setting up housekeeping for themselves. I wrote you last mail that I was a candidate for County Judge. My present prospects are flattering & if nothing unexpected takes place I shall be elected. I however have to contend against a strong democratic majority in this County, so that you see it is doubtful.

As to politics, I think there is no doubt but Buchanan will carry the State. Still great efforts are made against him. I'm for Fillmore. But I much prefer a Southern man with Northern principles to a Northern man with Southern principles. Buch's principles have always been the loaves & fishes. I also wrote you last mail asking you for a loan. I much want it, for I am in a situation where I shall

be obliged to make great sacrifices if I do not obtain it. I
pledge myself to secure it by conveying to you my entire
interest in a Canal which is worth three thousand dollars.
You may think it strange that I apply for this loan but I
cannot raise the money here unless upon a ruinous interest
& then it is difficult. I want also to take up a note of a large
amount against me & my former partner Edwin Gates who
is now at Long Island. This I can do with the indebtedness
of Adams & Co which I can buy at ten cents on the dollar—
When I wrote you some three or four months ago I supposed
that this note would have to be paid in cash, but now I can
manage it otherwise. If elected I much want to be placed in
a position to avail myself of passing events. If not elected to
place myself beyound the reach of absolute want. Elizabeth
send her love to all. Remember me to to [sic] your family
& to my old friends

Yours truly
Henry Eno

Campo Seco Nov 18 1856

Dear Brother

      Yours of Sept 30th was received a short time
since. I hope soon to receive a letter from Mary. If she dont
write soon I'm half inclined to write her a Spanish one. I
shall be much dissappointed if she does not write in French.
I have a curiosity to know whether she has made much
progress in the language. When Milton the poet was asked
why he did not teach his daughters the language he replied,
that he thought one tongue was enough for a woman. That
I think ill natured. I hope Mary will learn to speak & write
French well. I am also glad to know she is fond of music
and plays on the piano. Now I'm fond of music though I

dont know Hail Columbia from Yankee Doodle but there
is something in the "harmony of sweet sounds" that always
pleases me. You say perhaps she may sometime or other
teach Carrie. Swell, I like that—but then she will have to
come out here for at present I see no prospect of my going
there & as Carrie has now been with us almost sixteen
months we cant think of sending her off. I really dont see
why you cannot come & bring Eliza & Mary with you. You
have abundant means. You have worked hard enough &
long enough to entitle you to a play spell. Now Elizabeth
& I would think nothing of the journey. It would be a mere
pleasure excursion, but it is one we cant afford. I believe that
it is a well established fact proved by men of science (Fremont among the number) that it is no farther from the
Atlantic States to California than from California to the
Atlantic States. If this is so & I see no reason to doubt it
why not prove it by making the journey. This will reach you
in December probably—now by leaving in one week, you
avoid the hard winter that is something. It will be rather
novel to spend January, February & March without seeing
snow. You will see life as it is on the Pacific shores. The
day is not far distant when an Empire will be established
here. There is room enough. There will soon be men enough
& unless a Pacific Rail Road is built there will be nothing
to bind us to the Confederacy. Come & see for yourself. As
to politics, I wrote you I was a candidate for Judge. Well, I
got beat. Reason why, did not get votes enough. Our State
& presidential Election came on the same day & Democracy
ruled the roost.[22] This State has gone for Buch & Breck,[23]

22. After serving a four-year term as County Judge of Calaveras
County, Eno was defeated for re-election in the Democratic landslide
of 1856.

23. The candidates of the Democratic Party in the election of 1856

and so I presume have the majority of States. Pennsylvania the keystone state indicates it by her Oct Election. I voted for Fillmore,[24] though I thought he stood but little chance. As matters now are, I class the three candidates by degrees of comparison, Fremont Black R., Fillmore Blacker R., Buchanan Blackest R. My sympathies are for Fremont or rather for the principles of which he is the Standard bearer. Under Buchanan's administration I see no chance of a Pacific Rail Road unless it should be an extreme Southern route, which California does not want which will pass through inhospitable deserts & which will serve no other purpose under heaven than aiding the Chivalry by the expenditure of an hundred millions of dollars to fasten the chains still firmer on her Niggers & tickle some Northern doughfaces. I made a fair race. Beat others on the same ticket with myself and as defeated candidates always try to console themselves so do I, by saying that if there had been an intellectual & moral balance by which votes could be weighed instead of counted I should have beat my opponent out of sight but the mischief was the votes were counted. Well I'll make the best of it & try hard to have reason to thank God before the year is out that I was not elected. I look with considerable anxiety for a letter from you by next mail.

Elizabeth send her love to you & family. Remember me to all.

Yours truly

Henry Eno

---

were James Buchanan, President, and John C. Breckinridge, Vice-President.

24. Millard Fillmore was the candidate of the American Party in the election of 1856.

Wm Eno   Campo Seco Dec 18 / 56
Dear Brother
            Yours of Nov 13th is just received   I am sorry
that circumstances are such that you could not help me, but
I must make the best of it. I have held on to the hope that I
could so arrange my affairs as to avoid sacrificing some
property which is valuable as bringing me in a monthly income but which promises to be still more so in course of
time. The bad health of my wife prevents my doing what
I should otherwise do & by keeping me so much at home
paralyzes every effort I make. Her sickness during the time
I announced myself as a candidate for Judge & the election
in all probability was the cause of my losing it. I confess it
is rather mortifying to look back and find that altho I have
struggled hard to obtain a competence still I have failed &
have failed where many others have succeeded. If I every
[sic] had much of a stock of vanity it is much reduced at this
time. The future too looks dark but the present is what I have
got to do with. First I'm determined to owe no man   I will
sell within a short time what I have & pay to the last dollar
what I owe & secondly I'll not give up yet, but pick my flint
& try again. It is doubtful now whether I shall remain here
longer than spring but when I shall go I have not as yet
determined. With the money I recd from Fathers estate I
purchased an interest in a Canal (a small one) in Amador
County. I now own one third of it. It has cost me about
$2600 & is paid for. I am anxious to save this from the wreck
and to do so shall part with every thing else. To pay three
per cent Int per month is more than I can stand.
    Notwithstanding all my hard fortune I like the Country
& shall never leave it unless on a visit & I now see no chance
of that. I was truly sorry to hear of Lady's death. You did
not write whether she left children. Tell Mary I have not

received that French letter yet. My own health is good Elizabeth is about home. Little Carrie is well as usual.

My love to all.

                                    Very truly Yours
                                              Henry Eno
W Eno Esq

Wm Eno   Campo Seco Jany 18 1858
    Dear Brother
            Yours of Dec 9 was recd day before yesterday. I wrote to Mary last month in answer to a letter received from her. I am well. Elizabeth has been almost sick with a bad cold for the weeks past. Our little one has also been unwell for a couple of days for the first time in her life. The weather here has been so far mild & pleasant. Sufficient quantity of rain has fallen to enable the farmer to plough and a greater breadth of land will be put in grain this season than ever. The first frost we have had of sufficient severity to kill vegitables occurred on the 7th of this month up to which time we used tomatoes from our little garden. I am truly sorry to hear that Markus Culver has broken & still more sorry to learn that "he will not get up again"—to start in life rich & then to be reduced to poverty is harder than when poverty has been the lot from the first. To fail & to break down is nothing when a man gets used to it. *It is only to try again. A man has never lost all until he loses his courage. When he loses that he is irrevocably gone.* I am also sorry to learn that Myers was involved. I think your plan of winding up the affairs of your bank a good one & hope Congress will this year take the subject up & declare the issuing of all paper money unconstitutional.

    I recd a letter from Edward   he writes me that he is flat broke lost some $30,000. Was taken sick & con-

tinued unwell for four months that then he set about
straitening up his affairs & has paid about $20,000 of his
indebtedness leaving $10,000 unpaid but which he hopes to
arrange some way or other. He writes that Frank has gone
to Louisiana, that Edward is at College.[25] I receive letters
occasionally from Augusta. She writes me very good letters.
I think Edward has brought his family up well & that he &
they will eventually do well. I hope so at least.

I think of leaving here next spring but am undecided
where to locate   it is time I had settled down—
for time has left its impress upon me & I cant reasonable
expect it will show me many favors. It has so far however
dealt lightly with me. I am very glad to learn that the
financial whirlwind did not reach you. I sent Walter an
agricultural Address. You do not mention having received
it. Give my best respects to Eliza & the family.

Yours truly

Henry Eno

Sacramento California

April 11th 1865.

E. J. Eno Esq.
    Dear Sir
            Yesterday I received your letter of Feb. 22? Your
brother, Judge Henry Eno, was in the Hospital some time.
On the 3rd inst. he left here, for Markleyville, Alpine Co.
Cal.—with Mr. R. M. Folger,[26] who engaged the Judge to
edit his Newspaper, The Alpine Chronicle.

25. Francis, always referred to as Frank, was the eldest son of Henry's
brother Edward; he named his second son Edward. Both of Henry Eno's
brothers had sons whom they called Frank.
26. Robert M. Folger came to California in 1849. He established a
hardware and machine business in Sacramento, for a time in partnership

His health and spirits were very good, and he felt sanguine
of doing well and of being able to resist temptation.

The death of his wife and only child caused him much
affliction and sadness.

He spoke of his two brothers, and I think would like
to go to either of them, but that he was too proud to
be dependent. He seemed determined to again achieve independence by his own exertions. I hope he may succeed,
for I esteem him very highly.

I remain

Your obedient servant

G. J. Phelan M. D. County Physician[27]

---

with a man named Clift, and later with his brother, at 222 J Street between Seventh and Eighth streets. He once described his store as being
"on the northwest corner of the alley between J and K streets." After
his business was destroyed by fire, he became editor of a newspaper in
Sacramento and served as fire chief. *Romantic Forty-niners,* Daughters of
the American Revolution Pioneer Records, 1950, p. 166. *Sacramento
City Directory,* 1851. Calaveras *Chronicle,* December 27, 1851. *Sacramento Bee,* January 28, 1896.

27. Gregory J. Phelan, a well-known Sacramento physician, was a
charter member of the Sacramento Medico-Chirurgical Association in
1850, a promoter of the Sacramento Medical Society in 1854, and a
supporting member of the State Medical Society in 1856. He therefore
was associated with all of the early professional medical organizations in
the city. He served as physician to the cholera hospital in 1850. Between
1863 and 1870 he was County Physician and Superintendent of the
County Hospital, located on L Street between Tenth and Eleventh, and
it was in this capacity that he knew Henry Eno. Phelan was interested
in civic affairs, serving as a member of the Board of Education in Sacramento during 1858. He was an active participant in the Society of California Pioneers, holding the offices, at one time or another, of director,
president, and corresponding secretary. Joseph Roy Jones, *Memories,
Men and Medicine: A History of Medicine in Sacramento, California
with Biographies of the Founders* (Sacramento, Society for Medical Improvement, 1950), pp. 341–44.

Illinois State Sanitary Commission
Claim Department
Springfield, May 15, 1865.

Dr Brother

I received a letter to day from Dr G J Phelan "County Physician" Sacramento California dated April 11th. Stating that Judge Henry Eno had been in that Hospital, but on the 3rd had left there for Markleyville Alpine Co with Mr. R M Folger who had engaged Harry to Edit his newspaper.

The Doctor says Harrys health was restored and spirits good "that he felt sanguine of doing well and resisting temptation."

"The death of his wife & only child caused him much affliction & Sadness"

"He spoke of his two brothers and I think would like to go to either of them but that he was too proud to be dependent, he seemed determined to again achieve independence by his own exertions. I hope he may suceed for I esteem him very highly." I sincerely hope the Doctors wishes may be realised.

When last heard from the boys were all well   Frank was at Fort Barancas Pensacola.[28] Christina & Augusta are with me.

Yours truly

Edw I. Eno

28. Fort Barrancas was built by the United States between 1839 and 1844. Federal forces withdrew from this fort on the mainland in 1861 to Fort Pickens on Santa Rosa Island, which commanded the entrance to Pensacola Bay. Confederate forces held the Fort from early 1861 through 1862. Extensive documentation on the "Fort Barrancas Mili-

Wm Eno   Alpine Co June 22 1865
    Dear Brother   Markleyville.

I was very glad to receive your letter of the 21st
of May which arrived yesterday. I'll make no promises but
will try to answer all letters promptly. You say nothing of
Eliza or Frank. Hope they are well & enjoying life. My
health at present is very good. I have had two slight attacks
of Erisepelas but think I now know what to do for it. My
remedy is Iodine & starvation. You say you are not as active
as usual that is strange as you are only sixty four. Moses
who tried to emigrate to Palestine was I believe 120 when
he died & his eye was not dim nor his natural force abated.
I dont like to be asked how old I am. Told some young
ladies the other day who had the impudence to ask me that
I was so young when I was born that I really could not
reccollect. They all believe I am about sixty & I dont deny
it. To be old in a such a new country is a great sin & I am
trying to be considered one of the righteous. My hair is of
the color of the top of a mountain about a mile distant from
where I am writing & which has some of last years snow
on it. But to walk to Silver Mt distant 12 miles tires me &
to come back the same day to save the expense of staying
over night fatigues me, so I find my "natural force" is
abated. Was glad that you wrote me that Mary's husband
Capt Ellis was at Washington City. I have just wrote & put
a letter in the post office for him. Want him to try & get
$100 which Uncle Sam owes me for services in the office of
an Assessor of the Internal revenue. Right glad to hear that

---

tary Reservation," dealing primarily with Spanish land grant claims
and fort construction, can be found in Senate Executive Document 103,
41 Cong., 2 sess. 1869–70.

Edward's three noble boys have all got back safe and sound.[29] The true secret of passing a pleasant life is to secure happy memories. They must be in possession of it. I am in a new County high up in the Sierra Nevada, altitude over 6000 feet. Snow in winter two or three feet deep. Have not seen a flake of snow fall for several years before. The Carson river within a few rods of the house I live in, abounding in speckled trout. No fruit of any kind no country for agriculture or horticulture. Said & believed to be rich in Silver. About 60 miles from Virginia City & 120 from Sacramento, just on the line of the State of Nevada. It is now one of the poorest counties in the State, within a decade of years I honestly believe it will be one of the richest. I am something of a geologist & minearologist, can make an assay of ores as well as the best of Assayers. But I believe all mining countries have been & will be poor for the great mass of the people who live in them. I must make the best of it. If Capt Ellis receives my letter & if he should also receive & send me the $100 which is honestly my due I shall spend it in trying to be elected County Judge of this County. There are two ifs against me. I have my thoughts turned also in another direction. Congress has granted $500,000 appropriation for putting in a steam communication between San Francisco & China via the Sandwich Islands & Japan. I want to manage to go the first trip be a correspondent for some newspaper, give as interesting account as I can of all the incidents of the voyage & make up a book when I return about as truthful as travellers generally do. I believe I could make it a success & not draw more on my imagination than they generally do. This is a good country for a man who

29. At this time Frank, the eldest son, was 29; Edward, who went to Alabama during the period of Reconstruction, was 26; Stephen Henry was 24.

has his pockets well lined, but it taxes the ingenuity of the poor devil to the utmost to get what bread & meat nature demands & what clothes comfort & decency requires. I am editing the Alpine Chronicle[30] or rather writing for it. Would like the business well enough if it paid well. I dont spend two hours in a week. To keep from getting rusty have been reading Euclid & have now taken up the English grammar. Shall write to Edward to day. Give my love to Eliza. Remember me to Stewart Walter & Frank.

Yours truly

Henry Eno

I'll write to Frank *poco tempo* & tell him about grissley bears grouse speckled trout snow and silver &c.

H. E.

Wm Eno   Alpine County
Pine Plains   Markleeville July 24 1865

  Dear Brother

    I recd yours about ten days since of June 10. Delayed answering it to let you know the result of a Mass Meeting held here on the 22nd Inst. My health was never better. Living high up on the Sierra Nevada at an altitude of 6392 feet above the level of the sea we experience none of the sweltering heats of the Sacramento Valley & escape its debilitating effects. It has a bracing invigorating climate. Altho but 162 miles from Sacramento City it is here like living in a Northern Country, a few miles of longitude make

---

30. No issues of *The Alpine Chronicle* for the period of May–July 1865, when Henry Eno was the editor, have been located. The earliest issue preserved is that of June 16, 1866, located in the Bancroft Library, University of California.

many degrees of latitude in a mountainous Country. The coming Election excites a great deal of Interest in California not on account of State or National issues but because a U. S. Senator is to be elected & a Judge of The Supreme Court. It is men & not measures which now agitate politicians. We had in Alpine a convention which met at Markleeville on the 3rd   I submitted my name to the Convention as candidate for County Judge. There were three ballottings. I was ahead the first & second ballotting on the third was beat. There were five aspirants for the office. There was such a bargaining and selling of votes such a trading of offices that I would not submit to its decision. So with a few others got up a call for a Mass Meeting of the People, which was held last Saturday. I was there nominated by acclamation, so am a bolter, and accept the name. Shall try to be elected but acknowledge it is very doubtful. But am resolved not to lose the Election for want of energy & industry.[31] It is almost my only hope for what to do if I lose it I really dont know but dont trouble myself "for sufficient for the day is the evil thereof"

Your draft of $50 came in good time   enabled me to obtain a horse and go through the County. If the election should come off in Sept the same time as other candidates for office are voted for, should feel very sure of it, but Judicial offices are voted for in Oct. So I am afraid that at that I shall have to "paddle my own canoe" without having any one to take a side oar. I am no longer connected with the Alpine Chronicle as its Editor. I left it because they did not

31. According to the *Monitor Gazette,* July 8, 1865, there were seven names submitted to the Union Party convention for county judge: Robert Thompson, Henry Eno, I. Marshall, C. P. Goff, Moses Tebbs, Sextus Shearer, and H. Cook. Moses Tebbs of Silver Mountain was nominated on the third ballot.

use me well & I found that I should get nothing but my board. They now owe me over two hundred dollars of which I shall never obtain a dime. The proprietor wanted a nomination for Assembly, but could not get it. Is one of the incapables & without any moral worth. He begged of me to stay but I could not & obtain my own self respect, which is now what I look for & reckon more than that of the world. I know Judge Markee very well & it pains me to hear of the death of any of my old Dutchess Co acquaintances. I am sorry to hear of brother Edward's son Edward going to Mobile. It has been the graveyard of many a northern young man   better infinitely better go North to Minnesota or to some one of the new territories of the U. S. which will soon be knocking at the door of Congress for admission as independent States. I shall write to Edward to day. This County is now one of the poorest in the State   before ten years it will be one of the richest. It has silver enough in it to pay the national debt of the U.S. & the Copperhead debt piled on top of it & then have money enough left to buy hemp enough to hang every rebel in the Country. I went a few days ago to see several mines   wrote a letter for publication which when I receive the paper will send you. I formerly wrote a great deal for newspapers without pay, now I write for pay. But it is a dog's life to lead. Please write & tell me about Eliza. Is her health good? about Frank is he a good student? how tall is he? about Stewart, Is he agoing to be a millionaire? and has he a house full of children? I'd much like to see his girls. About Walter and his bairns. I'd like a word or two about John Couch & Harry Husted. About Harry Myers his children & grand children. About Wm Booth & in truth about a great many others. My impression is Stewart owes me a letter. He should not plead the statute of limitations. Also I want to learn something about Corine Love (?). With many grateful thanks for your kind letter & its enclosure I remain Your Affectionate brother

Henry Eno

If you and Eliza would come out to California & climb the Sierra Nevada to where I live I really believe it would give you both a new lease of life. And then too you would have something to tell your great grand children.

H. E .

Wm Eno   Alpine County
                                        Silver Mountain
Pine Plains   Aug 28 1865
Dear Brother

I wrote you sometime since that we had a convention for the purpose of nominating County officers, that I presented my name to the convention for County Judge & was beaten, but determined not to stay beat, so bolted. A mass meeting was called & I recd the nomination. The election for Judicial Officers takes place the 18th of Oct. I interest myself in the Election for County officers which takes place on the 6th of next month, trusting that those I help will assist me in return—I have recently taken a pedestrian trip over our Alpine Hills & have made up my mind that our ticket will be elected & that if my election took place on the 6th of Sept I too would be.[32] All I have got to do is to hold my own. That I shall strive to do. Was absent twelve days & had quite an adventure. Was directed to take a certain trail but missed it, got lost & about 9

32. In the final vote Eno led Marshall by 55 votes and Tebbs by 158. *Monitor Gazette,* November 4, 1865.

o'clock at night found myself *nowhere*. Concluded to put up
for the night   had some matches, built a good fire, for it
was cold, near the summit of the Sierra Nevada. I slept
sound until morning. Had nothing to pay for my nights
lodging. A walk of about a mile brought me to a mountain
tavern where a good breakfast reconciled me to the rather
hard lodging. I shall stay here for eight or ten days. This
place is the most prominent mining town in the County[33]
it is 7000 [feet] high up in the world. There is but one
lode that now pays. That turns out about $2500 per week.
Is apparently inexhaustible. Many others will soon be developed, in fact rich ore has been struck in two other lodes.
Two months ago stock in the I.XL[34] (I excel mine) sold for
$5 per foot now for $50. In two months more probably
$100. Ere long this place will be a theater for wild Cali-
fornia excitement, where fortunes are made & lost in a day.
A cool shrewd man with a few hundreds can turn his hundreds to thousands. Then when a reaction takes place it is
best to "stand from under"   If successful in my election
have no fears but I shall do well enough. If unsuccessful

33. Silver Mountain was first known as Kongsberg, a name bestowed
upon the region by a group of Scandinavian miners that prospected
there in 1858. The town had a population of around 2,000 in 1862;
the next year the name was changed to Silver Mountain. Four years later
Eno estimated the population at 350. Maule, *Contribution*, p. 27. See
also *Sacramento Daily Union*, August 4, 1863.

34. The I.X.L. was the mine that founded the Silver Mountain district. The claim of 1,000 feet was taken up in the spring of 1862 by
J. H. Williams and others. After tunneling about fifty feet they struck
a ledge 4½ feet in width. Carefully selected ore was worth an average
of $200 a ton although some went as high as $625 a ton. The stock
was held by San Francisco capitalists and in 1863 was difficult to obtain
on the market. The company declared its intention to build a mill but
had not done so five years later. See "Mining Summaries" in *Mining
and Scientific Press*, 1–23 (1860–71).

must do as well as I can. Having much at stake am resolved
they shall not take judgment against me by default. My
health was never better. My best regards to your wife children & grandchildren

Yours truly
Henry Eno

Wm Eno   Alpine County
                                              Silver Mountain
                                              April 24 1866

Dear Brother

Your letter of the 18th of March was recd last
evening. I assure you that it was very gratifying as showing
that I was not altogether forgotten—was also glad to hear
mention made of some old familiar names that death has
spared. Should like to know something of Harry Husted-
Booth, Taylor Woodin & John Couch—also of Harry Myers
& family—who did Mary Thomas marry—I forget, & what
family have they? How many children has Stewart & Walter
& what are their names? Is Frank a good student & how
tall is he? What is Mary's boys name & how old is he? is he
smart? I should like to know about Colman Bortwich's
(who married Prudence Eno) family. I believe he had a boy.
& how is Rose? how many children has Adam Strever &
what are their names? Sorry to hear Ben Strever is in
trouble. I hope you will extricate him. Glad to learn that
you went to Venango Co Penn, the great oil region.[35] It

35. Venango County, Pennsylvania, was the first county to produce
oil in the United States. Operations were first begun in 1854 with the
organization of the Pennsylvania Rock Oil Company to develop a
property in Cherrytree Township. In 1858 George H. Bissell organized
the Seneca Oil Company and leased a piece of land from the parent

does a man good to once in a while leave the smoke of his
own chimney. It would not hurt you much to come to California. Nothing enlarges a mans ideas & more effectually
removes prejudice than travel. But it also has its disadvantages—in many cases proves the truth of the old adage "A
rolling stone gathers no moss"   You say you would like
a description of the Country I live in. It would take more
time than I can now devote to give a full account of it &
would task your patience to read it. It is the Switzerland of
California. Its name, Alpine, is indicative of the Country. Its
western boundary is the west of the Sierra Nevada about
11,000 feet above the level of the Sea, running east to the
upper waters of Walkers river. Its western boundary is about
20 miles from the Big Tree grove. I believe I gave you an
account of it once. Trees 25 & 30 feet in diameter, which
were good sized saplins when Virgil & Homer wrote. The
climate is cold. Snow here at Silver Mt was four feet deep
on a level—& in a five minutes walk I can now get all I want
of it. Haven't seen a flower yet & only a stunted spear or two
of grass. I dreaded coming here but have on the whole spent
the winter about as comfortably as any I have passed in
California—showing that a mans comfort & happiness does

---

company on Oil Creek. Operations were started at Titusville under the
direction of Colonel Edwin Drake who struck the first oil in August
1859. Intense excitement followed with leases being taken on all available land in the neighborhood. Commencing at Titusville, the tide of
development moved up and down Oil Creek and along the Alleghany
River. Developments at Cherry Run furnished further excitement, and
between 1865 and 1866 several new discoveries were made. Venango
County became a great producing center. Marcel Mitzakis, *The Oil
Encyclopedia* (New York, John Wiley, 1922), p. 509. See also, Paul
Henry Gidden, *The Birth of the Oil Industry and Pennsylvania Petroleum, 1750–1872: A Documentary History* (New York, Macmillan,
1938).

not depend so much on Climate or even money as many
think. We are here about 7200 feet up in the world. The
main dependence of the people is on the Silver Mines, there
is some gold & some Copper. I think two or three of the
Copper Mines will eventually prove very rich. In Carson
Valley about 17 miles distant there is some agricultural land.
They raise a little wheat, some barley & oats & the best
potatoes in the world, tho small. So also on the head waters
of Walkers river. Silver Mountain is the County seat. Laid
out for a big town but is a small one, about 350 Inhabitants
all told, from every country under heaven, with a *small
sprinkling* of Yankees and Norwegians. Living is of course
high here $10 a week because we are high up & a long ways
from the low lands of Cal, from which we draw all our
supplies. It is about 100 miles from where I lived in
Calaveras. The timber is chiefly pine of different kinds, fir
tamaraks (not swamp), cedar, Mountain Mohagany, some
Aspen, no oak hickory maple, sycamore. Scarce a tree but
what is an evergreen. Game is scarce. A few black bear no
grissley. They are on the eastern slope. A few deer, hare
& grouse are rather plenty. A few silver foxes skins worth
from $40 to $70 a piece. Some white weasels skins worth
$5. Speckled trout abundant. A stray eagle once in a while
seen. Blue birds & robins abound. You asked as to my duties.
County Judges have jurisdiction in cases of forcible entry &
detainers, insolvency, actions to prevent or abate a nui-
sance   they have appellate jurisdiction in all cases coming
before Justices of the peace. They are Ex officio Judges of
Probate, have power to issue writs of Habeas Corpus Mandamus & can grant Naturalization papers. There is no
appeal from the County Court in civil cases—in that respect he is little autocrat. Justices have jurisdiction to $300.
I make it a rule to decide all cases according to my ideas

of right & wrong and not according to the ideas of any of
our Supreme Judges—for whom I dont have much respect.
I make the law bend to equity not equity bend to law. Jurisdiction in criminal cases all crimes short of murder & treason
—and I believe no Court tries any cases of treason—(none
having been committed the last ten years)—the County
Court is a Court of record. The office is for four years.
Salary $1800 payable monthly. Should be glad if I could
get it at the expiration of a year. On the first of May $600
will be due me. Have not received a dime yet—& have so
far lived on borrowed money paying 2½ per cent per
month. You will ask how I live? Well I board myself, rent
a house, cook for myself. Buy no clothes, wear my old ones,
and all I have would not bring a dollar and a half at a
paper mill. Am a good cook—having read Cooks voyages
years ago. Flour is $16 per hund, beef 16 cents per pound,
eggs 75 cents per doz., bacon & pork 40 cents per lb. Everything else in proportion, washing 25 cents per shirt & $4
per week pays my board. You perhaps want to know my
daily habits. I make it a rule to get out of bed when I wake
up, let it be what time of night or morning it is, make my
fire, wash, bake some corn bread or buiscuit from Graham
flour, each costing here more than superfine flour. I do this
for the sake of health. Cook some potatoes—my corn bread
beef or bacon with good butter costing only 75 cents per lb
& some dried apples cooked with a good cup of tea (no
coffee) makes me a first rate breakfast. Once in a while a
grouse bot [bought] of an Indian for fifty cents and occas-
sionally some speckled trout costing only the fun of catching
them makes the variety. Breakfast over by sunrise, I sit down,
generally read a chapter in the new testament. Write letters
if I have any to write. Take up the Supreme Court reports of
which there are 26 vols and pour over them for two or three

hours. Dinner tells the same story. Occupy some time in making a Synopsis of all decisions in relation to Mining & incorporations. Toward evening study mineralogy & geology. Read the newspapers & Atlantic Monthly at night & go to bed when I am sleepy. Always lay down about two oclock P.M & sleep fifteen or twenty minutes. This is my regular routine, have pursued it for the last four months, with the exception of about twice a week rambling over the hills or fishing in the afternoon. For the last year I edited the Alpine Chronicle. That is, wrote the leaders for it—but quarrelled with them because they would not pay me as they agreed to, so cursed & quit them. I have delivered several lectures here on Sunday evening which have been well received. Twice each week I strip off and wash all over with soap & warm water, then oil myself from head to foot with Olive Oil. Have been in that habit for a long time. The old antient Greeks and Romans used to do it, so also in the times of our Savior, and I believe that if people would do it, it would banish rheumatism & consumption from the world. Every morning before I dress brush myself for five or ten minutes all over with a large horse brush. I believe it as beneficial for a man or woman as a currycomb & brush is for a horse, but most of people take better care of a horse than they do of themselves. If I am the least unwell go without eating until I get well. Take no medicine, as I choose to die a natural death. About once a month go without eating a whole day. The fast days of the Roman Church were I believe instituted for Sanitary purposes at first, & then made religious observances. The going without eating one day has an excellent effect on me, makes my head clear and my spirits more boyant. Now all this I fear you will think dull & uninteresting. One thing however I forgot to mention. Two little girls one eleven the other eight years old & a little boy come to my room every morning read say a geography lesson & write & I have become very much interested with them. As I well know the power of bad habits I am earnestly striving to ascertain the power of good ones, and dont find it a hard task. There is with me the absolute necessity of having something to do all the time & I find the more I have to do the more I can do. But you will say I am old & should have rest care & quiet. I dont believe in it. As exercise strengthens the body so it does the mind. I have often heard our Father say "the used key was always bright" never was there a more truthful observation. I for one am determined to wear out not rust out—and old as I am intend to leave a name which no relative of mine shall be ashamed of & which perhaps they may be proud of yet. There is a work which the profession wants, the law in relation to Mining & Incorporations & I am conceited enough to believe I can supply it. At least I'll try.

This County is now in debt $22,000, including a debt of $10,000 to Amador from which it was taken. It has been most wretchedly managed since its organization,[36] but matters are looking better. I have induced the Supervisors to institute a reform which saves some $2200 a year. But I have thereby made three or four of the County officials very angry, but I care little for that, for the people are with me. At present I am the most popular man in the County but I know what popularity is. It is often gained without merit

36. Alpine County residents complained bitterly at being forced to assume responsibility for a portion of the Amador County debt in March 1864 when the new county was created. They argued that Amador County had never expended any funds in the area making up the new county. Alpine County was continuously in debt. Eno mentions the figure of $22,000 in April 1866; it had risen to $40,000 in March 1868. *Sacramento Daily Union*, February 18, 1864, March 7, 1868.

& lost with out cause, so it dont elate me. There is a new
Judicial District established this last Session. The salary
$4000. This district is composed of Mono Alpine Kern &
Inyo counties. The Gov appoints the Judge to hold until
next Judicial election.[37] I was told by many that if I asked
for it I could receive the appointment & I believe I could.
But then my necessary expenses would have been very great,
I should have to travel to Kern & Inyo two new Counties at
least 300 miles in a new unsettled mountainous country with
a wild reckless population & I thought I had better let well
enough alone. It would have broken up all my habits of
study & altho perhaps I could have saved more money
should have lost in the end. There is more honor in being
District Judge than a little petty County Judge. But I have
got to that age which is as in the game of whist when you
are in the nine holes—honors dont count. What I aim at &
what I want more than any thing else is to be able to own
the Hot Spring ranch of about 160 acres situated about 12
miles from here & about a thousand feet lower down in the
Valley. There is a beautiful stream of water flowing through
it abounding in spreckled trout. About 25 tons of hay (always worth $25 per ton and often $40) can be cut from it

37. The Sixteenth Judicial District embraced that part of California
lying east of the crest of the Sierra including Alpine, Mono, Inyo, and
Kern counties. Colonel Harvey Lee, newly elected assemblyman, sponsored the approval of a bill appropriating an $8,000 salary for a two-
year term of the new judge. Although the names of several Silver
Mountain residents were mentioned by the press for the post, Eno's
name was not listed. The Governor appointed Assemblyman Lee for
the two-year term until an election could be held, much to the annoyance
of some Alpine residents who complained of collusion. A few months
later, in August 1866, Colonel Lee was thrown from his buggy in Sacramento and killed. Theron Reed was appointed his successor. *Monitor
Gazette*, April 17, 28, 1866; *The Alpine Miner*, August 25, 1866.

& with comparatively a little expense a hundred tons could be made a year—it is in a vally with mountains a 1000 feet or more high on each side. But the great beauty & excellence of it is the Hot springs, about eight or ten springs in a half acre several of them hot enough to boil an egg—also an ice cold spring, so that the water can be made of what temperature you please. The water flowing from all & running together on the half acre would amount to at least 25 inches as miners compute it (which is water running through an orifice 25 inches long by one inch wide under a seven inch pressure) eighty acres of the land is first rate. No timber on it   on each side plenty of the best of pine cedar fir & tamarack. In the summer season it is a most delightful spot. It can now I understand be bought for a $1000. I'll have it if I can buy it for that next year   the man who owns it asked $15000 for it two years ago & I believe it will be worth that within five years—that is, will bring that. The waters are medicinal & many persons say they have received great help from them. I want it, as a place to retire to when my four years of office have expired if I should live so long (& I wont die to accommodate any body)—if I owned it now I believe I could pay three or four per cent per month on that first cost without making any improvements on it.[38] I look at this Country & its prospects coolly & without excitement   I am no longer carried away by feverish impulse. Its silver mines must bring it out. A more than a years residence here have made me acquainted with it & I

38. Eno may have referred to those hot springs in Alpine County later known as Grover's Hot Springs. Descriptions of these springs, which were highly praised, appeared repeatedly in the press. *Sacramento Daily Union,* August 13, 1863; *Monitor Gazette,* June 18, 1864; *The Alpine Miner,* July 28, 1866.

have been over it on foot in about every mining district and unless silver should lose its value entirely Alpine now one of the poorest is destined within a decade of years to be one of the richest mining counties in the State. I contemplate delivering a lecture on the Geology & Mineralogy of Alpine within the next five or six weeks & to have it published. Will send you a copy

My County warrants bear ten per cent Int per annum. I am trying to negotiate with an old friend in San Francisco E. D. Sawyer District Judge of the 4th Judicial District[39] which is part of San Francisco for a loan of money enough to pay the debts I have been obliged to contract here. My election expenses & living have involved me in debt about $325 & which I must pay or lose my standing here. To live hereafter I intend to become a Newspaper correspondent for either a San Francisco or Virginia Nevada paper &

39. Ebenezer Davis Sawyer came to California via Cape Horn, arriving in San Francisco on January 1, 1851. The following autumn he located at Mokelumne Hill, where he practiced law until 1854. He was a member of the county Board of Supervisors in 1853, nominated in that year as Whig candidate for the state Senate, and elected in a predominently Democratic county. He served in the legislature at Benicia. It was in these years that Eno and Sawyer became lifelong friends. Sawyer retired from California politics, went to Washington, D.C. for three years, and upon his return to California continued his law practice in San Francisco. He was elected judge for the Fourth District Court in 1863 and served a six-year term, declining the nomination in 1869. He was a distinguished orator. In 1886 he was Republican candidate for Attorney General of California. Oscar T. Shuck, *History of the Bench and Bar of California* (Los Angeles, Commercial Printing House, 1901), pp. 520–24. See also *Records of the Families of California Pioneers,* Daughters of the American Revolution of California, *10,* 507–11, located in the California State Library, Sacramento. In the Calaveras *Chronicle* between 1851 and 1853, Sawyer's card offering his legal services was published alongside that of Henry Eno.

think I can do it but am much afraid I shall have to sell my warrants for fifty cents on the dollar. However I shall try & get along until the first of July & then they must go for what they will bring. I am determined it is the last time I'll be forced [illegible words] for I have set my foot down that I *will* be $1200 better off at the expiration of the year —I owe in all about $1500 but all except $325 is outlawed & this I'll pay if I live four years. I consider them debts of honor—which with me is a tenfold obligation stronger than legal liability—I'll conclude this long disjointed disconnected epistle with saying I am in excellent health in better spirits than I ever expected to be—have strength & activity infinitely more than I have good reason to hope   can walk as many miles in twenty four hours as I am years old, or at least that I own up to—for I pass here for sixty & sixty one—though I have heard some one or two say that they thought I must be sixty two—it is a great crime in this new country to be old and I dont intend to own I am guilty of it—I commenced to write a short letter but this only shows how poorly we often keep the best resolutions

My best respects to wife children & grandchildren—to think I'm grand uncle throws a chill over me.

Yours Affectionately

Henry Eno

I send you a map of the County[40] HE.

---

40. Two maps of Alpine County were available in April 1866. "A map of the Silver Mountain mining districts. Including the territory of the proposed new County of Alpine," compiled by Theron Reed (San Francisco, H. H. Bancroft, 1864). 19 x 25 inches. Also a "Map of Alpine County and mining districts," by C. D. Gibbes, 1866. Nine miles to 3¾ inches. As the latter map had just been released, it is likely to have been the one that Henry Eno sent to his brother.

William Eno   Alpine County
                                         Silver Mountain
                                         Feby 25 1867

        Dear Brother
                In your last letter you asked me I believe what
sort of a winter we had here. I think this the proper time to
answer it. It commenced snowing in Nov & has been at it
ever since almost. Occasionally a rain to carry off what snow
fell, a few days of warm weather then snow again. Here at
an elevation of 7000 feet Sleighs have once in a while made
their appearance. Down in the valley snow seldom lasts
long enough for sleighing. A week ago last Sunday I broke
the Sabbath by walking to Monitor distant 8 miles. A Miner
wished the County Judge to give a certificate of works done
on a Tunnel owned by some persons in Schenectady.[41] On
Monday made a survey & certificate & in the afternoon went
to Boulder Hill[42] where some some friends had taken up a
claim for me, distant three miles. Stayed in their Cabin all
night & found that whilst I had slept all night it had snowed
all night. When morning broke found nearly two feet snow
on the ground. Started for Silver Mountain about 10 o'clock
came down Boulder Hill which is at least 700 feet high to
the main road. Had to break the road all the way to within
1½ miles of home. Stopped at a new Quartz mill just erected
got a good dinner at 2 oclock & found myself in my office at

        41. The Schenectady Gold and Silver Mining Company, owners of
the Tarshish Mine in Monitor. Raymond, *Statistics,* pp. 51–53.
        42. Boulder Hill was located in the Mogul District and was a dis-
tinctive location in Alpine County because some free gold was found
in the large boulders. The owner of one of these large rocks was offered
$20,000 for his treasure and refused it. The rocks assayed an average
of $62 a ton. *Sacramento Daily Union,* August 28, 1863 and January 19,
1864.

4 P.M. this was the hardest walk I ever made. But the next morning I was as well & felt as well as ever. I know how to take care of myself. As soon as I got home, pulled off my clothes brushed myself vigorously with a stiff brush, then oiled myself all over with sweet oil drank a couple of cups of warm tea & set by the fire heating my bare feet for an hour at least as hot as I could bear them & was all right with no sensation of fatigue or weariness. This walk from Boulder Hill to Silver Mt was full 8 miles, but the deep snow made it a hard one. I tell you this that should you be placed in like situation you might benefit by my experience. I am in the habit of using oil to bathe my limbs & have been so for several years & am a great believer in its efficacy. It has snowed for the last week nearly every day & it lies on the ground at least 5 feet deep on a level but the wind is fast making it *unlevel*. Considerable damage has been done by Avalanches or snow slides. One of the best dwelling houses in town has been crushed & knocked end ways. Fortunately no family was in it having moved out not long ago. The house stood in a dangerous situation & I would never have lived in it in the winter. I live near Silver Creek off from Main Street   nearly fronting is a large building called the Mammoth Hotel. The weight of snow crushed in the entire wing being forty five long & 22 broad. The Hotel was occupied by a Mr. Pilkington & family—the wing was unoccupied. No one hurt—several families have moved out of their houses to more secure places. There are only two main streets in town that I consider safe to live in when these thunderbolts of snow these avalanches come down.[43]

43. This storm of February 1867 was the subject of extensive comment. *The Alpine Chronicle* of February 23, 1867, reported: "The greatest snow storm in Alpine County within the memory of 'ye oldest inhabitant' commenced on Monday evening and continued steadily for

Mr. Pilkington has a nephew a young man by the name of Humphrey from Virginia a real dare devil who was with Sherman on his famous ride down South. This young man works in a claim managed by Pilkington at Raymond distant 4½ miles in the mountains. He wished to come home & started on snow shoes & came to the top of the mountain at the foot of which is the town—this mountain has always been estimated at 700 feet above town. The snow had filled up a ravine running from the top of the mountain to its foot making it to appearance perfectly smooth sailing & no trees or rock to be seen. He boldly started down many looking on to see him & down he came with the velocity of an arrow from a bow, steady & self possessed until within about 200 feet of the bottom there was jump off place which he could not see. His snow shoes slipped from under him & down he came making a leap of forty or fifty feet unharmed & ready for another snow slide. All the young men & all the young ladies are out every afternoon on their snow shoes.[44] In fact they are a necessity & without them there is

90 hours leaving a depth of snow in our streets of three feet [Markleeville]. The storm blocked all roads, and suspended all travel including the mail stages." The county sheriff finally made the trip from Silver Mountain to Markleeville on snow shoes in nine hours. He confirmed Eno's comments about houses in Silver Mountain being carried away by an avalanche and many others damaged by the accumulation of snow on their roofs. Additional articles on the weather appeared in *The Alpine Chronicle,* March 9, 1867.

44. Alpine County was one of the earliest centers of skiing in the Sierra. The name of Snowshoe Thompson heads the list of those who gained fame in this endeavor. Arriving in California in search of gold in 1851, he was ranching along Putah Creek in the Sacramento Valley three years later. In the fall of 1855 he fashioned a pair of skis out of valley oak and in January 1856 crossed the mountains from Placerville to Genoa, Carson Valley, Nevada by a route through Alpine County. This feat encouraged snowshoe activities among the miners in Alpine,

now getting about. We have had no mail for a week & it is doubtful if we have any for a week to come. I forget whether I wrote you that I was acquainted with J. Winchester[45] No 36 John St New York. I wish if you go to New York you would call on him. He intends to come out here next season. He was the former partner of Horace Greely, is a

---

Sierra, and Plumas counties. Competitive races were being run in the Sierra before 1860, and in the decade from 1860 to 1870 skiing became a major recreational activity in the mining camps. Numerous clubs and contests were organized. Among the most famous was that of February 1869, when Snowshoe Thompson and his "Alpine Boys" were defeated by the "Sierra Boys" who had developed a "dope" to grease their skis. Thompson maintained his reputation for cross country travel but not for speed. Robert H. Power, *Pioneer Skiing in California* (Vacaville, Calif., Nut Tree, 1960). For a specific reference to Alpine County activity, see *Sacramento Daily Union,* March 7, 1868. Snowshoe Thompson became a public figure interested in politics and his name is repeatedly mentioned in the Alpine County newspapers of the 1860s.

45. Jonas Winchester and Horace Greeley established *The New Yorker* in March 1834, which six years later became *The Tribune.* Later Winchester established the *New York World* as a vehicle for the republication of standard works of literature and science in an inexpensive form. Early in 1849 he started for California, and in March 1850, at San Jose, was elected state printer. In 1851 he moved to Grass Valley where he built the first saw and quartz mill in that vicinity. In the 1860s he speculated in mining claims in Alpine County. Returning to New York, Winchester owned and operated a patent medicine business that produced "Winchester's Hypophosphites." Prior to coming back to California in 1872, he attempted to promote the Globe Gold and Silver Mining Company, capitalized at $650,000 in shares of $10 each, to develop a property at Monitor. Winchester was the president, managing director, and trustee. *Sacramento Daily Record-Union,* March 7, 1887. Additional information may be found in the Pioneer Biographical Cards, and in approximately 240 items of the Winchester Papers, in the California State Library. See also *Some Facts About Gold and Silver Mines and Mining, also the Prospectus of the Globe Gold and Silver Mining Company* (New York, J. Winchester, 1872). Pamphlet in the California State Library.

man of much intelligence & great enterprise he is extensively engaged in mining enterprizes & I hope to make his
acquaintance useful both to him & to myself. I last wrote that
I had my thoughts bent on Arizona but I shall conduct myself here in the same manner as if I had determined to stay
here for life. I shall go if I think I can better myself. A man
has just called & says he is going to carry the mail out on
snow shoes so must close

Very truly Yours
Henry Eno

Alpine County Markleeville
April 1 1867

Dear Brother
    Wm Eno
        I left Silver Mountain about a week ago & have
been rusticating at Markleeville.[46] Shall probably return

46. Markleeville was named for John Marklee, who settled there in
September 1861 and built his cabin on the site of the future town. In
August 1863 the town was described as "a very bustling, thriving little
township on the banks of the middle fork of the Carson River." Markleeville was more compact and better built than Silver Mountain and
possessed the advantage of good roads. The roads leading to Placerville
and Genoa ran through the town, and no less than three six-horse
stages arrived and departed daily. One correspondent reported: "The
little town of Markleeville shows an illustration of Yankee go-aheadness.
Commencing business a year ago with a couple of small shanties, it can
now boast of nearly one hundred dwellings and stores." There were
nearly fifty families there in August 1863. Besides stores and workshops,
there was an opera house where a corps de ballet, consisting of a half-
dozen "Teutonic coryphees, alias hurdy-gurdy girls," and a famous jig
dancer from San Francisco performed every night in the week. Admission was free, but the fee for a dancing partner was four bits plus the
cost of drinks. The town boasted the only dry goods store within ten
miles, and a brewery was in the process of construction. By January
1864 the population of Markleeville was 2,620. There were 168 build-

tomorrow. I wrote you some four weeks since a sort of snow
storm letter & it has snowed almost every day since. Silver
Mountain has been blockaded so completely that a stage
coach has not been in it for the last seven weeks. The mail
has been brought in on the snow shoe line two or three times
a week. Here nearly a thousand feet lower the snow is about
two feet deep, except in the roads which are bare, so it is
neither sleighing or wagoning & wretched walking & miser-
able riding.[47] Seventy miles west grass is green & flowers in

---

ings in the town, including a well-equipped mill of fifteen stamps.
Over $200,000 had been invested in buildings and equipment, one-third
of which was in quartz mills and mining machinery. The town moved
forward rapidly during the winter because freight trains could travel
to Markleeville with supplies but could not go on to Silver Mountain or
Monitor. The town was known locally as the head of "whoa-haw" navigation. By February business lots were being sold from $200 to $1,000,
and lumber cost $40 per thousand. In addition to its dry goods store,
the town had five wholesale and retail grocery and provision stores,
three hotels, three clothing stores, one drug store, two blacksmith shops,
two shoemakers, two breweries, four saloons, one fruit store, and one
tobacco and cigar store. There were eight lawyers, three physicians,
and a minister in town. Among the fraternal orders, the Masons and
Order of Odd Fellows were active. Markleeville had replaced Silver
Mountain, the county seat, as the emporium of the county. However,
Monitor was emerging as the rival community, and in February and
March of 1864 its citizens subscribed labor to assist road contractors who
were trying to open up the stage road from Genoa beyond Markleeville
to their town. *Sacramento Daily Union,* August 13, 28, 1863, January
19, February 1, 18, 1864.

The Alpine Chronicle, March 30, 1867, confirmed: "Judge Eno has
also been rusticating among us during the past week. He returns to his
mountain home on Monday. It is pleasing to have our friends from the
mountains visit us and enjoy our balmy Spring weather."

47. The comparative advantages of transportation to Markleeville
and Silver Mountain and the nature of "whoa-haw" navigation were
discussed by *The Alpine Chronicle,* March 23, 1867. The newspaper
commented, "The mail and express matter now pass between this place
and the county seat on snow shoes."

blossom. At San Francisco they have green peas & straw-
berries. Here snow, sage brush, & silver (when they find it)
& they are still on the look out for it, by mining long tun-
nels & sinking deep shafts. The summers heat & winters cold
makes no difference. I am as sanguine in my belief that success will crown their efforts eventually as ever but as I told
you in one of my letters I am determined to leave next fall
for Arizona unless I find myself in a much better condition
than I am now financially. I however do not intend to be so
unwise as to leave a certainty for an uncertainty. Here I
have $1800 a year & can live on it. By uncertainty I mean
a haphazard adventure. I must run some chances, but I am
taking all reasonable measures to have the probabilities in
my favor. I am asking for a federal appointment, but dont
depend on it. I expect to practice my profession & to make
my living by it. In looking back to see the various moves
I have made with the hope of bettering myself I find that
among the mistakes I have committed was that I had not
located at the seat of government. That was the great mis-
take I committed in Iowa   I should have settled at Burlington   so in California I ought to have gone to the
seat of Government or to San Francisco. In going to Arizona
I intend to go to Prescott the Territorial seat of Government.[48] In the course of a few years the territory will be
knocking at the door of Congress for admission as a State.
The resolute man will not bend to circumstances, but make

48. If Eno had moved to Prescott because it was the seat of government for Arizona Territory, he would again have misjudged the situation. By the time he could have reached Arizona, the capital had been
moved to Tucson (1867). A land office was created at Prescott in that
year, but the territory was attached to California as a surveying district.
Land surveys began in 1868. Even so, Prescott's population fell to 500.
Anne Merriman Peck, *The March of Arizona History* (Tucson, Arizona
Silouettes, 1962), pp. 163–70.

circumstances bend to him. There may be chances there which are not here for me & I'll try & profit by the past. But in the mean time I will act & do in every respect as though I intended to remain here permanently. I am authorized to sell two silver Mines & I hope to find a purchaser this summer

for that reason I wrote to J. Winchester 36 John St NY. I shall as soon as I have held my Court in June go to Calaveras & try once more my fortune in Gold hunting. Five years ago I engaged in an enterprise which I had to abandon because of the trifling circumstances of expending all my money & exhausting all my credit. I then thought I was right & will try & prove I was the coming summer. I have also a claim of 200 feet in this County which has cost me nothing so far, & I think so well of it that I would not exchange it for any other in the County but if every thing fails that I have engaged in I shall certainly go to Arizona. I have perhaps but few years to live & I will make the most of the best of them. At least I will try. I'm determined not to wait for something to turn up but try & turn up something.

I should like if you go to New York to have you call on Mr Winchester. He writes he will be out this coming summer. I'll write to Frank as soon as I go home. My health is very good & I hope this will find you & family well

Yours truly

Henry Eno

Alpine County   Silver Mountain
April 12 1867

Dear Brother

I write you frequently because the blockade which the snow instituted still continues, for I believe more than eight weeks no stage has come into Silver Mountain, on

Sunday of this week I received a telegram requesting me
to go to Monitor[49] distant 8 miles. So left on Monday
& made my way easily enough on a beaten trail remained
there two days & went then to Boulder Hill distant two
miles. Staid there all day & night with a couple of miners
working a claim in which I have an interest. During the
night it snowed & in the morning I found the snow knee
deep & more coming, they tried to persuade me to stay but
I resolved to go back to Silver Mt. Boulder Hill is so high up
in the world that in going down to the road I found in
twenty minutes walk the snow not more than six inches
deep. I travelled on the road very easily about 4 miles, then
had to use the Hill, every rod the snow was deeper. About
a mile & a half from my home I stopped at a Scotchmans
near the quartz mill & got an excellent dinner & a cup of
tea. I again set out. The driving wind had covered up the
trail & I went leg deep in snow every step. I believe I rested
almost every rod for a mile. It grew deeper & deeper worse
& worse the sleet almost blinded me. I deliberated what to
do. There is a creek running near the road all the way. I
turned & went down to the creek & followed the bed of it
up to town knee deep in many places. I was just two hours
& a half in making this mile & a half. Stripped off my
clothes rubbed & brushed myself down most thoroughly,
then oiled myself all over with sweet oil, set by the fire &
baked my feet for an hour went to bed at nine o clock &

49. Monitor came into existence as a mining camp later than Silver
Mountain and Markleeville. The settlement was located on the banks
of a tributary of the Carson at the foot of Monitor Mountain. Monitor
gradually drew population away from Silver Mountain after 1865. Production from the Tarshish mine caused the town to flourish briefly in
1868. The population was 300 in 1872. Maule, *Contribution*, p. 27.
See also *Sacramento Daily Union*, August 28, 1863, and *Daily Alta
California*, July 24, 1865.

slept without waking up until broad day light in the morning. To day feel as well without any stiffness or soreness as
I ever did. I have made out to borrow $800 on the pledge
of $2187 in County warrants. This about pays all I legally
owe in the world. I am to pay 3 per cent Int per month & pay
it all by the 15th of Nov. & I'll try & do it or sell my County
Warrants for what they will bring. I wrote you about my
going to Arizona. I am determined to do so if by next Oct
or Nov my prospects are no better. Recent events have
brightened up things here wonderfully. The Washington
mine at this place can in the course of one month keep a
ten stamp mill running,[50] i.e.—can crush ten tons of rock
& amalgamate it per day. The IXL claim near this place is
being worked. I live with the superintendent & they admit no
one but the workmen into their mine. About a year & a half
ago there was taken out some $18 or 20,000 but the lode
pinched out. The Superintendant now tells me that they have
a well defined lode of 8 feet wide of the very richest kind
of ore. If so (& I have the utmost confidence in him) it will
not only make the stockholders rich but inspire confidence
in this Silver mining region. I can now buy the stock at two
or three dollars per share. If he tells me truth (& I know he
does) it will go up in the hundreds. I have said I could buy
stock for two or three dollars per share if I had the money.
But I have not got it & have strained my credit about as
much as it will bear. This strike is not now known & prob-

50. The Washington Mill Company processed the ore of the I.X.L.
in the Silver Mining District. On one occasion the milling company
contracted to pay $1,000 a ton for 100 tons of first-class ore from the
I.X.L. Browne, *Resources,* pp. 170–73. Eno claims the negotiation was
for 100 tons at $100 but that the I.X.L. management refused the con-
tract. Eno rather than Browne must be correct on the amount offered
a ton because the Comstock lode at Virginia City averaged $45 ore.
See Henry Eno to William Eno, July 8, 1867.

ably will not be for four or five weeks. At Monitor they have recently struck a Silver lode called the Tarshish[51] which I went into the tunnel & saw. It was fully eight feet wide & the richest silver ore I ever saw. Two or three assays have been made as high as $500 & $700 to the ton. They are not through the ledge & dont know how wide it is. The telegraph operator here says he received a telegram this morning that the ledge was twelve feet wide & that ore that had been taken to Virginia City assayed $1400 per ton. This strike in the Tarshish lode will create a great excitement & when it is know that the IXL lode has a rich ledge we may expect all the Mining Speculators all the Mining Sharks & reckless adventurers to come prowling among us. I have been through a good many feverish excitements & know the premonitory symptoms. It may be spasmodic but I think it will become chronic in Alpine Co. I have written to J Winchester today he lives at 36 John Street & has written that he will come out here this coming season. I much wish you would come with him. He is a very intelligent man courteous & well bred & having lived in California you will find his company not only agreeable but perhaps advantageous. I recd a long letter from Augusta Eno Taylor. She writes like a lady or what is better like a good woman. I'll answer it tomorrow.

Yours truly

Henry Eno

51. The Tarshish, at Monitor, had been located some years before and in the late 1860s belonged to the Schenectady Gold and Silver Mining Company. Discovery of a new ledge in 1867 created a great deal of excitement. Production figures of Alpine County mines are usually contradictory; this is particularly true in the case of the Tarshish. In 1868 Lewis Chalmers, a well-known assayer from England, ran ores from the mine and reported values at $1,000, $2,000, and $200 a ton. Yet in 1869 the mine produced only $8,360 in bullion, reduced at

Wm Eno   Alpine County
                                            Silver Mt
                                          May 15 [1867]

    Dear Brother

        I write you frequently because I wish you to keep
posted as to how I am & also as to events occurring here.
I feel interested in them & therefore presume that others
do. I am well & prize health enough to adopt the means
to preserve it. For six long years the people of Alpine Co
have persevered in their endeavors to develope their Silver
Mines. Last year was a gloomy time. But day is beginning
to break & the dark clouds that have hung over our snow
clad hills are about being dispelled. I wrote you about their
striking a rich lode of silver in the Tarshish tunnel at Monitor. They are now in over 24 feet & no indications of being
through the ledge. This claim is 1000 feet in length. As
they progress in crossing the lode the rock is richer & richer.
7½ tons were worked at the Ophir Mill in Washoe Valley
& yielded over $350 to the ton. The average of the Com-
stock lode thought to be the richest in the world is not over
$40 to the ton. This Tarshish lode promises fair now to take
precedence of the Comstock, & Alpine County bids fair to
be one of the richest Mining Counties in the state of California. You will of course think that I have given up my
Arizona expedition. By no means. If I stay here I will have
more business as County Judge and no more pay & I cant
live as a County Judge should live on $1800 payable in
County Warrants which are at a discount of at least fifty

Davidson's Mill on Silver Creek. At the same time first-class Tarshish
ore was said to run $300 a ton. See "Mining Summaries" in *Mining
and Scientific Press*.

cents on a dollar. I'm paying now $24 a month interest money & I live as economical as possible, board & cook for myself & wear clothes scarcely decent. I'll go to Arizona or to the Devil sooner than stay here if there is no better prospect before me next October. But I'll strain every nerve & use every exertion to better myself pecuniarily. Here I enjoy the best of health & I would not barter it for wealth.

At Silver Mt there is a mine called the IXL (I excel) which has also struck a very rich lode, but they try to keep it secret. But have got so many to help keep it that it has leaked out. I see the symptoms of another feverish mining excitement, but dont see how I can avail myself of it. I see the road to fortune but cant travel it because I cant pay the tolls. To catch a big fish requires a small one for bait & I haven't even a minny. Before this reaches you, you will have probably received a letter of introduction given by me to one Willson. He can tell you all about the Country & the Mining prospects. I have also written to a Mr Winchester No 36 John St N.Y. & to a Gen James F Hall No 15522157 [?][52] Broadway N.Y. informing them that you contemplated coming out here & thought you would be glad to accompany them. They have probably written you. I should be much pleased to once more see a human being to whom I am related especially a brother & will do all in my power to render your visit to this land of snow & silver pleasant & profitable. I go tomorrow with the Clerk to Monitor distant 8 miles from there to Markle[e]ville & to Woodfords[53] to

52. General James F. Hall of New York was president of the Active Silver Mining and Tunnel Company. He arrived in Alpine County in October 1866, to assume control of the company's affairs. *The Alpine Miner*, October 27, 1866.

53. "Register Your Name. Judge Eno and County Clerk Barber will be in Monitor on Thursday next; at Cary's Mills [Woodford's] on Friday, and Markle[e]ville on Saturday for the purpose of registering the

enable persons to have their names registered as voters. I
go on foot shall be gone four or five days   it is a 50 mile
walk but I dont heed it. What a dignified situation a County
Judge occupies when he has to walk 50 miles on Official
business because he is too confounded poor to hire a horse.
You wont blame me for thinking seriously about Arizona.

Best respects to wife & family

Very affectionately Yours

Henry Eno

(written in haste)

Wm Eno   Alpine County
Pine Plains   Silver Mt
                                                  May 31 1867

Dear Brother

This will be forwarded to you by B Pilkington[54]
a near neighbor & friend of mine   he returns to Sandoval

---

names of voters. Let every Union man see that his name is on the
Great Register." *The Alpine Chronicle,* May 11, 1867. See also *Silver
Mountain Bulletin,* May 18, 1867.

Woodford's was a hamlet built by John Carey at the site of his sawmill in 1853 or 1854. Daniel Woodford was his partner, and when he
acquired full possession of the property the name of the settlement was
changed in 1869. At the junction of the Carson Canyon and Markleeville roads, it was an ideal location for the way station known as Woodford's House. Maule, *Contribution,* p. 27.

54. B. Pilkington, Esq.'s name was continually in the newspapers of
Alpine County in connection with mining promotions and public
affairs. See for example *The Alpine Miner,* December 2, 1867, for his
comments on the Raymond District in general and the Illinois and
California Company in particular. He was also a great orator who spoke
at Markleeville on the occasion of the 49th anniversary of the Odd
Fellows Lodge. *The Alpine Chronicle,* May 2, 1868. He was a candidate
for the California assembly in 1867. Calaveras *Chronicle,* May 11, 1867.

Marion Co Ills to attend to interests which he has there, &
contemplates again returning to this place in the fall. He is
extensively engaged in mining in this County, or rather in
developing Mines & with a fair show of ultimate success—
he will forward this letter from New York City & if he
remains in the City a short time will append a note informing you how long he will be in the City & where to be found.
I wish you could make it convenient to visit him. He knows
every thing about the mining interests of California & is con-
versant with its agricultural & commercial interests. I am
certain that I would go 120 miles to see any one from Pine
Plains. So I hope you will do the same to see one from
Silver Mt   I have written to Edward at Springfield Ills,
& to Frank his son at St Louis requesting them to call on him
at his home at Sandoval.

Mr Pilkington is a gentleman whose acquaintance is worth
cultivating, and one in whom implicit confidence can be
placed.

Yours truly
Henry Eno

Silver Mountain
July 8 1867

William Eno
Dear Brother
I recd a letter from you about ten days ago—
which is unaccountable mislaid. When I opened it I was in
hopes to have learned that you was about starting for California but to my great dissappointment not a word was said
about it. You barely mention that you would see Mr Winchester. I recd a letter from him of May 21 stating he intended again visiting California but set no time. My health
is first rate, in fact better than for many years past. When

I say better, I mean that I feel stronger more active & have more of the youthful feeling than I have had for years past. I attribute it to the life of strict temperance I lead, to obeying all the laws of Hygein & to the exhiliarating air of this mountain region & perhaps also to the total want of care for the preservation & safe keeping of my worldly treasures. I am rather more comfortable situated now than I have been since my residence in Alpine Co. As Judge of the *highest Court* in California & I believe in the U.S. I have hitherto employed a County Judge as my cook, but have discharged him & now have employed a "female woman." In other words an old acquaintance one Tom Hay went to Canada & brought back a wife. They occupy the house & I board with them. I hope to continue the arrangement but it is uncertain. I wrote you that I applied to the District Court for a Mandamus to compel the County Treasurer to pay me monthly. The District Judge decided against me. I have carried the case to the Supreme Court & I hope to get a decision this month. If decided in my favor I shall remain here if against me I shall go to Arizona or the D—l—

The mines are promising fair. The Tarshish mine at Monitor 8 miles distant is a wonderful rich mine. It is said three men can take out ten thousand dollars worth of Silver ore in a day. The IXL mine at Silver Mt is also very rich. They were offered $100 per ton for 100 tons of ore but would not take it. The average of the famed Comstock lode at Virginia City is only $45 per ton.

We had a celebration of the 4th of July here & I was called upon for an oration. So I gave them a sort of *spread eagle speech* which passed off very well I believe.[55]

---

55. A systematic search of California newspapers has revealed no comment or quotation on this oration. *The Alpine Chronicle* at this

The weather has been very fine for some time past, the days warm the nights cool. The deep snows of last winter are not all melted as yet. The mountains look like the head of a man of middle age here & there patches of white. One Mountain looming up in the distance looks like mine all white. Within rifle shot of where I am writing is a deep snow bank.

I dont like the political complexion of things. I think Horace Greely has made an ass of himself. Instead of a Greely he has shown himself a *greeny* or a Granny. Government are trying to prove the truth of what is said by some one that "Great crimes are great glories." The indomitable energy with which the four years war was conducted is giving way to imbecility—the truth is, it requires infinitely more talent to conduct the affairs of government in time of peace than it does in time of war. But the people have not found it out yet & I am afraid never will.

I see you are all alive about your rail road project. I'm afraid when you have got it it will prove like the Elephant the man won in a raffle. We expect the Pacific rail road to be completed in 1870 & I hope to take a ride on it then. It took me six months to come across the plains. Who know[s] but what I shall return in six days *"nous verrons"*

My love to wife & family

Yours truly

Henry Eno

---

time was located in Markleeville rather than Silver Mountain. *The Alpine Miner,* July 6, 1867, reported that July 4 had "passed off very quietly here, no public demonstration." At Silver Mountain there was a picnic and ball that was well attended, but no mention was made of Judge Eno's remarks.

John R. Woods, Sec.   ILLINOIS CLAIM DEPARTMENT,
Edward I Eno, Agent

Springfield, Ill., Aug. 19th 1867.

Office, South-East Corner of the Square
opposite the American House.

Wm Eno Esq

Dear Bro. I have just returned from a visit to
Sandoval Ill. to see a friend and near neighbor of Harrys—
B. Pilkington—he is the Agent of a Mining Co of Chicago
who are developing a Silver Mine in Alpine Co Cal. Mr B.
[P.] owns a peach orchard of 12000 trees at Sandoval & has
come to attend to the sale of his crop. I found him a very
pleasant & intelligent gentleman and a warm friend of
Harry. He says Harry is a remarkable Man for his Age,
Mind & body vigorous as any young man & fills his Office
of Judge with with Much credit to himself. "Financially he
is not well off" but he has some Shares of Stock in Companies that may yield very large, as they have struck two
of the richest Mines in the world. But at present & probibly
for a year Harry will be Oblidged to sell his County Scrip
which he is oblidged to take for his Salary so that it will not
nett him only about 40 cents on the Dollar. And that the
best investment his friends could make for him would be
to take his scrip & loan him money enough to live on for a
year, when in all probibility it will be paid. Now I have but
little to spare but I will send him $50 if you will send him
$100—and in Six Months $50 more if you will send another $100 and charge him 10 pr ct Interest. I think it will
do him good. He seems to be discouraged because he cant

get his salary. If you conclude to send him I will send you a Draft on New York for my share.

Capt Taylor is making the New Storm Co a complete success.

Yours truly
Edw I Eno

General Depot of
Winchester's Hypophosphites and Specific Remedies,

36 John Street.
New York, Jan. 10th 1868

Dear Sir:

I made the acquaintance, years ago in California, of your Brother Henry; and have corresponded with him since my return two years since.

I have to-day a letter from him, dated 15th Oct. at Silver Mountain, in which he repeats the request that I would write to you, in regard to Mining and other matters of interest. He says you have talked about making a trip to California, and he would be glad to have you do so, in my company, if possible.

It is my intention to sail in about two weeks, on my sixth trip to the Pacific, for the purpose of opening and working a *Silver Mine* of which I am two-thirds owner, and President of the Company.[56]

In my opinion, based upon many years of observation and

56. Jonas Winchester actually had interest in two adjoining mines, the Winchester and the Globe, which ran south from Monitor Canyon into Silver Hill, or Mount America. Winchester wrote a series of articles appearing in the New York *Tribune* in April 1869, chiefly on the wonders of the Monitor District where he held mining claims. His statements were so "highly colored" that the newspapers of Alpine

experience as a practical miner, there is no field of Enterprise in which hundreds can be converted into thousands so soon or so surely as in judicious Mining investments.

Were you disposed to examine into the matter, I could offer you opportunities such as are rarely to be met with; and where the investment would all be returned in less than a year, while the Property would be quadrupled in value by the developments.

A few thousand in the hands of your brother, would I believe, insure him all the wealth that a reasonable man could properly ask for.

Should you have any word to send to your Brother, or package of any kind, I should take pleasure in being your messenger.

Begging your pardon, if I have trespassed upon your time, with things of no moment to you; and with cordial good wishes.

I am yours very Truly

J. Winchester

Alpine County
Silver Mt
Feby 13 1869

Dear Brother

Yours of the 13th of Dec was received a short time since. You say the last letter of mine you received was dated Dec 9 1867. I have *certainly* written since then. I also wrote

---

County, and even the *Virginia City Enterprise,* published protests. For the controversy that ensued, see *The Alpine Chronicle,* May 1, 1869, and *The Alpine Miner,* April 17, 1869.

a long letter to Frank & well recollect some time after writing to you & complaining that he had not answered it. The dull routine of last year has not been relieved by any good fortune or good luck extended to me. But I have no reason to complain. I have long since learned that it is of no use to grumble. Grumbling is the poorest use a man can put his breath to. My general health has been good with the exception that I had what Doctors call a Carbuncle on the back of my head. I left here on the 24th of June for San Francisco, hoping to obtain a better situation for myself. On the way I found that I had what I supposed a boil on the back of my head. I went by the way of Campo Seco my old residence. A Doctor there told me it was a Carbuncle & cut it open. I was aware that I must have better medical advice than I would get there & hurried to San Francisco. Called upon Doct Toland[57] the most eminent surgeon in the place. He pronounced it a Carbuncle & must be more thoroughly opened. Made what he called a crucial incision. Three days after made another. The amount of it was that I was under the Doctors hands six weeks & suffered incredible pain. Several old friends called on me during the time. During

57. Hugh Huger Toland, a Carolinian trained in medicine at Transylvania College, Kentucky, and in Europe, came to California at the time of the gold rush. After the death of his wife in Stockton in 1850, he went to Calaveras County and became an owner of the Gwyn [Gwinn] mine at Mokelumne Hill. Both Henry Eno and E. D. Sawyer were there at the time, and the men undoubtedly were acquaintances, if not friends.

In 1853 Toland sold his mining interests and returned to San Francisco, where he launched a brilliant career in medicine. He was named physician and surgeon of San Francisco County, appointed surgeon at the United States Marine Hospital, served on the first board of health in San Francisco, and founded Toland College, which he transferred to the University of California in 1873. He was appointed Professor of Surgery and first president of the medical faculty in the University. It was generally agreed that he had the largest and most lucrative medical

the time I was under no concern but what I should get well, but was afterwards told that no one thought that I could survive. I called on an old friend of mine a Doct Holbrook who visited me every day for a long time. I got well in spite of all predictions & no ill consequences have resulted except a heavy medical bill & board bill & losing all chance of obtaining what I went for. I wanted to go to Japan as a correspondent for a Newspaper & should have obtained a good situation, but another was employed during the time I was confined to the house. The person I was in treaty with supposing that I would not get well. I returned to Alpine with intention to leave it as soon as I saw even a remote chance to better myself by so doing & I am disposed to take great risks. I cant live here & make any thing more than a bare living & I live more economically than any other person in the County. I receive a County Warrant for $150 each month, worth in market only thirty seven & a half cents on a dollar. I have acted as Judge here a little over three years. About $750 dollars of my County Warrants have been paid, but not to me. I have been obliged to part with all I have so far received, so that when I leave the County it will trouble me to raise $200. And leave it I shall, & that within two months. You have read in the papers I suppose about White

---

practice in California, amassing a fortune. His skill as a surgeon has been considered phenomenal. Hubert Howe Bancroft, *Chronicles of the Builders of the Commonwealth*, 7 (San Francisco, History Co., 1892), 271–84. Henry Harris, *California's Medical Story* (Springfield, Ill., Charles C. Thomas, 1932), p. 134. Alonzo Phelps, *Contemporary Biography of California's Representative Men 1882* (San Francisco, A. L. Bancroft, 1882), pp. 33–36. *The Bay of San Francisco: The Metropolis of the Pacific Coast and Its Suburban Cities,* 2 (Chicago, Lewis Publishing Co., 1892), p. 586. *San Francisco News Letter,* 30 (April 24, 1880), p. 12. *The Americana . . . Biographies* (New York, Americana Corp., 1929), p. 68.

Pine. It is about 350 miles east of here & is a rich Silver Mining locality.[58] I have made arrangement with three friends of mine to go with them & to leave here between the 1st & 15th of April. We go with a wagon & horses & two or three pack animals. I should have went immediately after my return from San Francisco but could not raise the requisite funds. After I arrive at White Pine shall be governed by circumstances. In 1850 perhaps you reccollect that I went to Los Angeles & from there 240 miles east to work a gold mine in the Desert. This was one of my wild goose adventures. We found the mine we were in quest of worked it for two months & abandoned it. It was a gold mine & in a Limestone formation, the only one I ever heard of in California. One of our Company a Tom Davis, one day came in & said he had found a Silver mine & showed us some Silver ore. Said he had traced the ledge over three miles & that if it was in Mexico it would be worth a Million of dollars (he Tom Davis had been in Mexico & had worked at Silver Mining) but that then & at that time it was worth nothing. Tom Davis went away that week. I went & found a ledge answering his description. The Gold mine we worked & this ledge that Tom Davis said was Silver is on the same Meridian of Longitude that White Pine is. Ross Brown[e] in his report to Government on the Mines[59] says that Silver

58. Jackson, *Treasure Hill.*

59. J. Ross Browne prepared a report dated November 24, 1866, that was published as *Letter to the Secretary of the Treasury, Transmitting Report upon the Mineral Resources of the States and Territories West of the Rocky Mountains* (Washington, 1867). This 321-page report was printed in *Reports Upon the Mineral Resources of the United States* (Washington, 1867), which also included a "Collection of statistics upon gold and silver mining east of the Rocky Mountains," by James W. Taylor, pp. 323-57. Browne mentions the Pahranagat District on p. 134. The next year Browne published a longer *Report on the*

is found at Pahranagat in Limestone which is about 100 miles north of where I was. The White Pine Silver Mines are in Limestone, so that it appears this Limestone mineral bearing belt extends several hundred miles. I want & intend to explore the Country lying between White Pine & this Gold mine I worked. This Gold mine is about 40 miles north of the Sink of the Mohave river. After we had abandoned the Mine we went to the Sink of the Mohave & stayed there two or three days. We had in our company two men one an Indian the other a Mexican, we had hired to take care of our horses & mules. We were all well armed except the Indian. He made himself a bow & arrows—one day he shot at a large bird sitting on the dry limb of a tree. He missed the bird & lost his arrow. He told the Mexican to go & stand where he thought the lost arrow had probably fell & he the Indian went back to where he had stood & shot another arrow at the place where the bird sat. The Mexican watched where it fell & by that means found both. I am going to do as that Indian did shoot another arrow in the

Mineral Resources of the States and Territories West of the Rocky Mountains (Washington, 1868). This publication by the Government Printing Office again contained a short report by Taylor. H. H. Bancroft and Co., San Francisco, printed an edition under the same title but with the Taylor contribution omitted. A third printing of the report was released by D. Appleton & Co., New York, under the title *Resources of the Pacific Slope* (1869). Taylor's statement for the government report was again omitted and approximately 200 pages added: "A Sketch of the Settlement and Exploration of Lower California," "Sketches of Washington Territory," and "Sketches of Nevada." Thus the 1866 report of Browne was published twice in 1867, and the second, or 1867 report, was published three different times between 1868 and 1869. Eno undoubtedly was referring to one of the printings of the second report for there is a thorough discussion of the Pahranagat District, pp. 426–29. Francis John Rock, *J. Ross Browne: A Biography* (Washington, Catholic University of America, 1929), provides helpful bibliographical information.

same direction. When I came to this Country I kept a journal. I shall keep a journal of my route & incidents occurring & perhaps some day give it to the world in the shape of a book, Twenty Years on the Pacific Slope. I know I am not as young as I was twenty years ago, but all the iron in my composition is not yet smelted out. I have the same love for adventure. I have hardihood & power of endurance which few men of my age have. I well know I am not nor ever have been prudent, but I have enough prudence to avoid & shun the quick sands & rocks on which I have been stranded. There are times when even audacity is prudence. I've nothing but life to lose & every thing to gain & in life so far as I have had experience there is but little to enjoy & much to endure. It is then wisdom to know how to enjoy a little & to endure much. I presume you have given up the idea of coming to California. Some time next summer the rail road will be completed. Your rail road through Pine Plains has occupied your time & attention I suppose. When completed you can visit your Mary at Yonkers without trouble between sunrise & sunset. I should imagine it would increase the value of your property having such easy access to New York. I really hope the institution of rail roads will be of some service to the Country at large. I believe they will eventually—but for a time they will contribute to build up great cities (which are great sores) at the expence of the Country. I am going to Carson City in a few days. Will write you as soon as I return. When I leave here shall give directions to have my letters forwarded, so I hope you will write & address as usual.

Feb 13 / 69

My kind regards to Eliza & Frank. Remember me to such old relics as may survive & who remember Harry.

Yours truly

Henry Eno

Nevada
Carson City
March 2 1869

Wm Eno
    Dear Brother

        I came to this place which is the Capital of the
State of Nevada about a week ago, intending to return immediately, to Silver Mountain, but am detained waiting for
a man I wish to see who will not be back for a week yet.
So to save expense of travel concluded to remain until his
arrival. The Legislature is now in session & from several of
the Members I am enabled to obtain information respecting
the State & as my attention has been particularly directed to
White Pine my enquiries have principally been to that locality   I well know that New York papers have made
you somewhat acquainted with the excitement which the
discovery of Silver ore has created & therefore suppose you
would like to hear from me respecting it. White Pine is
about 300 miles distant from this place, directly east. I
have seen many persons from there & they all unite in in
saying that it is almost fabulously rich in Silver ore & much
of it worth from two to fifteen thousand dollars per ton.
Over two millions of dollars worth of bullion have been
shipped from there within the last three months. The ore
is found in a sort of limestone formation, very different
from Silver ledges in Alpine Co. The ore is found in Deposits
of great extent & not in ledges or lodes as in other localities.
It is believed generally that the section of country in which
this ore is found was once covered by the sea & it is part of
what is called the great Basin. Treasure Hill on which is
the famed Eberhart mine is 9000 feet above the level of the
sea. The snow in winter is very deep & weather cold but

in the vallies near by cattle can obtain good pasturage all the year round. Chloride flat below Treasure City also contains many mines, the ore very rich. The chloride of Silver is an evidence that the Country was once covered with Salt Water for chloride of silver is formed from the mixture or blending together of salt & Silver. I am well acquainted with Gov Blaisdell [Blasdel] of Nevada[60] & at his invitation spend much of my time in his office. He has invested all his means there, has an interest in the mines & is engaged in erecting a Quartz mill. The Gove made a fortune of $100,000 in the famous Comstock mines, but got rid of two thirds of it & confidently expects to recover all losses & make the hundred thousand a million. The fact is half the people here are more than half crazy & perhaps you will think I am for the White Pine fever will take me off in six weeks time. I however have nothing to lose so I'm on the safe side. From present indications I believe there will be twenty five or thirty thousand people in the vicinity of White Pine this coming season.[61] Of those some few will make

60. Henry Goode Blasdel, first state governor of Nevada, came to California in 1852 via the Nicaragua route and became a farmer in the Santa Cruz region. He moved to Virginia City, when it was still a part of the Territory of Utah, and engaged in mining and milling operations. He became superintendent of the Potosi, Hale, and Norcross mines. In 1864 he sold his interests and returned to his native Indiana. There he became interested in politics and represented Nevada on the committee of the National Union League that notified Lincoln of his renomination. Returning to Nevada, where the state constitution had been adopted in his absence, Blasdel secured the gubernatorial nomination at the Republican convention. He was re-elected in 1866 for a four-year term. While governor he devoted a large portion of his time to mining promotions and speculations. *National Cyclopaedia of American Biography, 11*, 200. See also "H. G. Blasdel, Nevada's First Governor, 1865–1870," *Nevada Highways and Parks, 22* (November 1, 1962), 18–19.

61. Eno's estimates of the size of the White Pine mining rush are more exaggerated than most, although some guide books and promo-

fortunes & many, very many, make failures. I may make
a fortune one thing is sure I cant mar it. I shall return to
Silver Mountain hold a court on 18th of this month & hope
to get off by the middle of next month & expect to camp out
for the next four or five months. Hope you will write &
address as usual for letters will be forwarded to me.

My love to Eliza & Frank. I really think Frank ought to
write to me.

Very Truly Yours
Henry Eno

Health very good. Weighed today. Found I bore down 173
lbs. At least ten pounds too heavy.

Monitor Alpine Co
Wm Eno   May 26 1869
    Dear Brother

        I wrote you some time ago that I intended leaving
this County & going to White Pine. Should have left before
this but the want of means prevented. Have recently made
two trips to San Francisco & back involving great expense,
but was compelled to do it. On my return found that I must
stay & hold my Court the first Monday of June. Now hope
& expect to be off by the 15th of next month. If able I shall
go by rail road to Iowa & St Louis this fall—perhaps spend
the winter there. I am beginning to have a sort of home-
sickness what the French call a *male du pays* I want once

---

tional literature mentioned a potential population of 40,000. In the
winter of 1868–69 the entire population of the White Pine District was
between 2,500 and 3,000. With the coming of spring the population
soared to an estimated 12,000. According to the 1870 Federal Census
the three towns of Hamilton, Treasure City, and Shermantown had a
combined population of 6,765.

more to see some one connected to me by ties of blood. I am not as young as I once was, I am beginning to find out but dont fear the journey overland. Regard it more as a pleasure trip than otherwise. Have learnt this much of philosophy, never to borrow trouble & when trouble comes, shake it off as soon as possible. The completion of the Pacific R. R. enables us to talk by means of letters & I hope to hear from you frequently. I'll write every week until I leave & often after. I am staying a few days at this place but shall return in a short time. My love to your wife & Frank.

Yours truly

Henry Eno

Alpine Co

Carey's Mills

Wm Eno June 18 / 69

Dear Brother

I left Silver Mountain on Monday of this week— have been waiting all week for a letter which I hope I have reason to expect will contain the means to enable me to leave for White Pine. Now think I shall stay there but a few weeks and find my way the best I can to St Louis & Fort Madison. My term of office expires next Jany. I tell the people here that I shall be back & hold my Oct term of Court, but may perhaps dissapoint them. My office can be declared vacant by my leaving the State one month, so if nothing better offers shall return, but am on the look out for the chances. My health is very good & give myself but as little trouble about the future as possible. If good, it will be well & good, if bad I'll make the best of it.

Very truly Yours

Henry Eno

Let your next letter be addressed to *Treasure City White Pine Co Nevada* hope you will write on receipt of this. Tell Frank to write also. June 21. I missed sending this by Saturday's mail. No letter from Sacramento as yet. Am waiting with as much patience as I can, but have not much stock on hand. Weather delightful. Trout fishing good. This letter starts on its journey east tomorrow the 22nd. Expect you to receive it in ten days. Shakespeare makes one of his fairies Partha say "I'll put a girdle round about the earth in forty minutes", the telegraph may beat it yet. Received a letter from Augusta wife of Capt Taylor of St Louis & judge they are all doing well. Ed & Capt Taylor had the White Pine fever. It was only spasmodic not chronic as mine is. Have recd half a dozen letters from White Pine. One or two urging me to come. It is a wild country with a wild reckless set of adventurers in it, but I'm used to both. I've kept out of the pale of civilization so long that I am afraid I could not stand it for only a short period. Intend spending next winter on the Colorado but dont always carry out my intentions. Must be governed by circumstances

H. Eno

Hamilton, White Pine

Wm Eno   June [July] 14 1869

Dear Brother

Arrived in this land of sin sagebrush & Silver on the 3rd of this month in good health. My first impressions are that this is the richest silver mining district discovered since Columbus discovered America. Went a few days ago to Robinson district, distant 45 [miles] to the east. Rode there in a waggon. Had a terrible dusty ride. Stayed there two days. Came back on horseback. Left at 8 in the morning

reached Hamilton[62] at 9 PM. Stood the ride well   rather
sore & tired but felt as well as ever next morning. Five years
of life in the health giving hills of Alpine have given me
wonderful hardihood & powers of endurance. This is the
very paradise for speculators & adventurers, men who have
some money & some sagacity. But rich as the Country is
there will be many more failures than fortunes made here.
All the capital I have is brains & they have not been worth
much heretofore. I am camped out opposite Treasure City,[63]
in a bush covered tent with few conveniences for writing &
have some dozen letters to write so this letter must be
brief   tell Frank to write me. Will write again soon

Yours truly
Henry Eno

Hamilton White Pine

William Eno   Aug 8 1869

    Dear Brother

        Your last letter was recd a few days ago but is not
at hand to refer to. Have been staying this three days at
Hamilton. My home if home it can be called is opposite
Treasure Hill about a mile distant & is a bush tent. You ask
me to give you some account of this White Pine Silver
region. It is difficult to describe to one who has [not] seen
a country like it. Nevada is a State abounding in Minerals of

---

62. Hamilton was the supply and milling center of the White Pine
Mining District. The town became the seat of county government and
the largest community in eastern Nevada during the years of the boom
and immediately thereafter. It was located at the base of Treasure Hill.

63. Treasure City was the mining center just below the crest of
Treasure Hill, 1,200 feet above Hamilton.

every description. It is in what Fremont calls the Great Basin. But if it is a basin there are a great many inequalities in it, this basin is elevated above the sea from three to thirteen thousand feet   there are several rivers, the Humbolt Carson, Walker & other smaller rivers all of which bury themselves in the sand   there are very many vallies widening out into plains bordered by Mountains, presenting a desolate appearance not clothed with trees as in the Atlantic States, but only here & there in the gorges. The timber is pine tamarack fir & Mountain Mahogany, all evergreens. The nut pine is the breadfruit tree of the indians, the nuts being very nutricious an[d] the principal food of the Indians. The mountains are mostly in the direction of N & S. of course the vallies are. Water is scarce & the traveller occasionally perishes with thirst. The vallies are covered with Sage brush & bunch grass. No trees, except an occasional cottonwood & willow where water is to be found. At the the base of the mountains springs are found the water of which is soon buried in the sandy plain. I know nothing so cheerless as a ride across one of these vallies of ten or twenty miles. Steptoe valley to the east is over 150 miles in length. This Silver region is dissimilar in many respects to any other in the United States. There is a limestone silver bearing belt extending four or five hundred miles in length & perhaps three hundred in breadth. Silver is found in the Northern portion and Gold & Silver in the Southern & about 80 miles east of here Gold is also found. That this Country was all once covered with the sea admits of no doubt. I have a small collection of fossils & shells gathered near where I am camped at an elevation of eight thousand feet above sea level. Hamilton where I am now writing contains about 2000 Inhabitants   Treasure city a thousand feet higher

has perhaps 1500. Shermantown[64] about as many. Then
there is Eberhart City[65] Swansey[66] & I believe two or three
others. Take Treasure City for the center there are perhaps
8000 within three miles of it.[67] I believe almost as many
more in the various mining districts within fifty miles. There
are about a dozen quartz mills within four or five miles, now
running 155 Stamps   each stamp can crush one ton of
ore a day[68]   it is impossible to say what is the average
yield of Silver to the ton. I put it at $50 to the ton but many
think more. Many tons yield from $1000 to even $10000

64. Shermantown, originally known as Silver Springs, was two miles
southwest of Treasure Hill, with a road from Hamilton leading down
a deep canyon to reach it. It became an important milling center and
the third largest community in the White Pine District.

65. Eberhardt City was located at the foot of Treasure Hill on the
south side in Applegarth's Canyon. This milling center was on a flat
adjoining the Stanford Mill. It had one hundred inhabitants in 1868
and 1869. After the British established the Eberhardt and Aurora
Mining Company and purchased the Stanford Mill, the town began
to flourish.

66. Swansey was just three-fourths of a mile north of Shermantown
and the site of a Swansea furnace, erected by an experienced Welsh
miner who had successfully operated a similar plant at Oceana in Hum-
boldt County, Nevada. The town became a bone of contention between
Treasure City and Shermantown and was eventually absorbed into
Shermantown.

67. Eno's population estimates were surprisingly accurate according
to the census of the following year.

68. Other estimates of milling facilities in the White Pine District
confirm Eno's impression. Early in the summer there were reported to
be ten mills working; at the close of the working season there were
fifteen. The total number of stamps were reported to be between 120
and 185. James D. Hague, *Mining Industry,* Vol. III in Clarence King,
The United States Geological Exploration of the Fortieth Parallel, Professional Papers of the Engineer Department, U.S. Army, No. 18
(Washington, 1870), 437. See also *White Pine News,* June 15, October 10, 1869.

per ton. There is much of what is called base or refractory ore here which cannot be successfully worked without roasting in a furnace or smelting, and several smelting works are being put up & I predict that in a few years there will be hundreds of smelting works established   Many very many handsome fortunes have been made here the last year & many have lost. The principal fortunes have been made by those who had money to start with. It is a Homopathic principle that like cures like & here the like begets like. But still there are a good many instances where poor laboring men have made what they call a lucky strike. The owners of the famous Eberhart mine were two years ago poor men, they are now millionairs. Gove Blaisdel [Blasdel] of Nevada is said to have realized $200,000, Gov Stanford & brothers,[69] as much more. Their position & capital have been turned to good advantage. The California bank of San Francisco is a great operator, owns a valuable mine & has a twenty stamp mill in operation. The climate so far as I can judge is cooler in Summer & colder in Winter than in California owing to its greater elevation. It is not a grain country though I believe wheat can be successfully cultivated. Corn will not do well here. As a pastural Country it is perhaps not equalled in the U.S. millions of sheep & cattle & horses can be raised & in the Southern portions of The State would find grazing all the year round & even here it is said Sheep & cattle can feed & do well all winter in the deep vallies where grows a kind of white sage that after frosts come cattle & sheep

69. Asa P. Stanford represented his brother Leland in many mining investments in Nevada and Utah. The Stanford brothers had purchased an interest in the Eberhardt Mine and had erected a mill in the district, which they sold to British investors. The Stanfords made a practice of buying up promising mining claims near the route of the Central Pacific, or projected branch lines, and selling them to capitalists in the East or abroad.

can feed of. At the elevation of from 6 to 8000 feet the
snows fall deep, in the vallies lying but a short time. There
is but little game here some few deer. On the crests of the
highest mountains Mountain sheep are found, hare & rab-
bits & doves abound in many parts but not many here. A
few grouse & sage hens. The grouse resemble prairie chick-
ens, sage hens are as large as our domestic hens. A company
are engaged in bringing in good water to Hamilton &
Treasure city at a great expense.[70] They have to raise the
water 800 feet & then carry in in iron pipes to where it is
wanted. Water is sold here at from 8 to 10 cents per bucket.
Where I am camped we have to pay 15 per gallon. I believe
the mines or at least the great majority of them will be as
permanent as Silver Mines in other parts of the world   I
have not abandoned the idea of returning to the Mississippi
this fall & shall do so if I can raise the means. Chicago sent
a delegation of some of her principal citizens to California,
they have been here. Among them was G. C Bates who I
knew at Sacramento more [than] 15 years ago   he is a
talented able man & spent over a week here. I told him I
designed to return this fall & give a series of lectures on the
industrial interests of the Pacific coast, its agriculture Commerce Manufactories & Mining but to make mining a spe-
cialty. He encouraged me & told me that if I would make
my debut at Chicago I should have as large an audience as
I desired & further said he would go with me to Detroit &
introduce me there where he was well known. I shall try

70. The White Pine Water Company pumped the water of Illipah
Springs, three miles east of Hamilton, up the side of the Mokomoke
Range, through a tunnel at the crest, down the other side, through
Applegarth's Canyon into Hamilton, and eventually to Treasure City.
The promoters expected to supply a community of 40- to 50,000 when
they invested $400,000 in the elaborate works. For a full discussion, see
Jackson, *Treasure Hill*.

to do so. I promised him I would, but it will depend upon circumstances. I left Alpine Co. without resigning my office. Have been absent now so long that the Supervisors can declare my office vacant & I presume they will. I paid every debt before leaving & had made arrangements so that I thought I should have eight or ten hundred dollars but through the falsehood & treachery of two men was disappointed   I have now some $1200 in County Warrants drawn for my salary. Unless I can obtain $500 I cant go for I'll not go east absolutely pennyless—I'll not be a dependant on relatives or friends as long as life lasts   should I go to the Mississippi I should return next spring   Mr Bates assured me that my lectures would be well received & would pay well & could I but make one fifth of what he said I could I should not hesitate   in the meantime I am engaged in preparing them   I wrote to Walter a short time ago & hope he will answer my letter. My health continues good and am in much better spirits than almost any other man in my situation would be & I am sometimes afraid it is a proof of recklessness rather than of cool philosophy. This has been written at one sitting, I have exhausted my paper & will close. Respects to Eliza & Frank

Yours

H Eno

Hamilton White Pine

Wm Eno
Aug 21 1869

Dear Brother

Yours of the 11th Aug was received yesterday. Have now been here since the 3rd of July. I came here expecting to find a rich mineral Country also to find much such a population as California had in 1849 & 50. The great

mineral wealth of Eastern Nevada has not been exaggerated.
In fact I did not expect to find so rich or so many Silver
Mines. There is not so much wild reckless extravagance
among the people of the towns & the miners as in the early
days of California. There are not as many homicides according to the numbers, but there is perhaps more highway
robberies committed. We have here as twenty years ago
numbers too lazy to work but not too lazy to steal & some
too proud to work & not afraid to steal. The laws of Nevada
license gambling & here at Hamilton, in Treasure City &
Shermantown are some ten or twelve licensed gambling
tables. The next session of the Legislature may perhaps
license Highway robbery. There are two banking establish-
ments, two Express offices, Wells & Fargo, & Union Express, some ten or twelve Assay offices & a small army of
Lawyers. The District Court has been in session ever since I
arrived. A trial often occupies ten or twelve days. A very
few Lawyers are doing well. From what I can discover I
believe that Lawyers depend more upon perjury & suborna-
tion of perjury than upon principles of law or precedents.
Experts in mining do a thriving business as Witnesses
there are I judge nearly two hundred paying mines within
four miles square. There ought to be a dozen more quartz
mills erected & would find full employment. The price of
crushing & working ores is too high for low grade ores.
The common price is $30 per ton. Under ordinary circum-
stances free ores yielding $15 per ton can be worked at a
fair profit. There are very many mining districts within 80
& 100 miles that are now attracting attention of miners &
capitalists. The Merchants of Chicago are turning their attention to this Silver Country & will enter into competition
with San Francisco & I should not be surprised if they succeed in establishing & building up a heavy business & a

profitable one. The money market in California as well as
in Nevada is very stringent. There is much financial distress.
Very many men reputed to be worth their many thousands
last spring are now reputed worthless. But in no country
that I have ever seen (not even in California) do I believe
that well directed industry & judiciously invested capital
would meet with richer rewards. It will never be considered
a good grain country, but as a pastoral country it is un-
questionable a good one. Millions of sheep can be kept here
& without cutting hay for winter. It is also a good dairy
country. There is a great scarcity of water it is true, but
Artesian wells can supply it. It is also a healthy country, no
fever & ague. At this high elevation persons of weak lungs
are subject to pneumonia but a little care will prevent it.
It is *no money* not *pneumonia* that I am troubled about &
am afraid it will become chronic. I went out a few days ago
with a young fellow on a prospecting trip, about four or
five miles from here. Went over as rough a country as I
ever travelled over   Stiping mountain is but a mole hill
compared with ours   on our return struck a Silver lode.
Brought home some specimens & had them assayed. Send
you the assay, so that you may see how we manage here.
Intend to prospect it further.

Have made up my mind to go to Iowa & St Louis if I can
possibly raise the means the fore part of Oct. & return in
the spring. I made the acquaintance of Judge G. C. Bates of
Chicago who was here a short time since. I formerly knew
him in Sacramento. He tells me I can make money by lecturing, advises me to make my debut at Chicago & that he
will introduce me. And also at Detroit. Am now busily engaged in preparing several lectures, but I labor under many
disadvantages   still hope to over come them. If I can but
put my foot on the lower round of fortunes ladder & grasp

with my hand another I have faith to believe I can yet climb
it.

Was pleased to hear about your farming operations.
Reapers mowing machines gang plows & the threshers have
found their way to the Pacific coast. Between Elko & Hamilton there are several mowing machines at work. Almost all
the wheat of California is harvested by machines. Last year
a Mr Mitchell[71] on the San Joaquin plains raised fourteen
thousand acres of wheat & this year Bidwell,[72] of the Sacramento Valley candidate for Gov last year raised twenty seven
thousand acres of wheat. Last year in June I was in San
Francisco. A farmer living near Sacramento river told me
that he had fifteen hundred acres of wheat which would
yield on an average 30 bush to the acre. He said he could
harvest it, thrash it, put it in sacks & store it in a warehouse
in San Francisco within a fortnights time. There have been
fifty six harvesting machines employed this year on the
Salinas Plains. I crossed them in 1850, & there was not a
furrow turned. Our markets here are well supplied with

71. This is probably a reference to Adolphus Mitchell, a successful
rancher of Tulare County, who came to California in 1855. He worked
for daily wages in Sierra and Mariposa counties, then signed on as a
cowboy on a ranch in Tulare County in August 1857. He started accumulating land in 1860 and in time had 1,280 acres under irrigation
southwest of Visalia and 1,500 acres of ranch land in the foothills six
miles north of Lemon Cove. J. M. Guinn, *History of the State of California and Biographical Record of the San Joaquin Valley, California*
(Chicago, Chapman Publishing Co., 1905), pp. 589–90.

72. Information on Bidwell's ranching operations is extensive
through his own accounts and those of others. Two items on Bidwell are
of special interest: a three-volume scrapbook, compiling scattered bits
of evidence, prepared by Charles C. Royce, *In Memorium John Bidwell*,
and a typewritten manuscript by Rockwell D. Hunt, "The Prince of
California Pioneers," an address delivered in Chico, California, on the
occasion of the Bidwell Centenary, May 19, 1941. Both are in the California State Library, Sacramento.

everything man wants to sustain life and some of the lux-
uries. Flour $8 per hun, beef & mutton 15 to 20 cents per lb.
Sugar three lbs for a dollar, bacon 30 cents per lb. Apples
peaches apricots nectarines & grapes from California in
abundance, all about 25 cents per lb. Potatoes 10 cents per
lb, beans the same & water 12½ cents a bucket. Seven
dollars a day for a horse to ride. I find it cheaper to go afoot.
Wood $6 per cord. Rents all the way from $40 to $400 per
month for one or two rooms. Plenty of good air but of rather
a light quality, nothing.

I think you would like a trip to this wild country & to the
more civilized portions of California. It would give materials
for thought & reflection & would in all probability enable
you to enjoy with a greater zest the comforts of a quiet
home. As for me I feel as if I had no Country & no home,
but try to make the best of it where ever I am. Shall be much
pleased to hear from Walter & how little Harry[73] comes on.
Best respects to Eliza, Frank & Stewart & Stewarts girls. I
would like a letter from them.

Very Truly Yours
Henry Eno

Alpine Co
Silver Mt
Sept 24 / 69

Wm Eno
    Dear Brother
            You see by this letter that I have returned to
Silver Mt   I found that unless I was here on the 23 Inst

---

73. Walter, son of William Eno, named his first son, Harry, after
Henry Eno, whom Walter had always known as Uncle Harry.

Alpine Co
Silver Mt
Sept 24/69

Wm Eno

Dear Mother

You see
by this letter that I have returned
att Silver Mt — I found that unless
I was here on the 2? Inst my office
would be declared vacant — so
left Hamilton on the Stage for Elko distant 110 miles — had a hard
dusty ride of 27 hours — did not get
in in time for the cars — had to stay
over untill next morning then took
the cars to Wadsworth stopped to see
S, W Knapp my nephew who is a
telegraph operator there — got there
at 12 oclock at night — left the next
morning on the freight train for
Reno arrived there at 11 A. M. I at
4 P. M. took the Stage for Carson City
Stayed there over the Sabbath I next
day took the Stage for Silver Mt
I reached there at Sundown —

my office would be declared vacant, so left Hamilton on the Stage for Elko distant 110 miles. Had a hard dusty ride of 27 hours. Did not get in in time for the cars. Had to stay over until next morning then took the cars to Wadsworth stopped to see S. W Knapp my nephew[74] who is a telegraph operator there. Got there at 12 o clock at night. Left the next morning on the freight train for Reno arrived there at 11 A.M. & at 4 P.M. took the Stage for Carson City. Stayed there over the Sabbath & next day took the Stage for Silver Mt & reached there at Sundown. I thought it best to return but it cost me two months Salary   I have to make such sacrifices on my County Warrants. I wrote to a friend in Sacramento that I intended to return. He invites me to visit him & deliver a lecture on White Pine Co. I propose doing so.

There is to be an election for County Judge this fall. I can be elected if I choose to be, but I do not want it. The Salary will be only $1000.[75] I like White Pine & intend to try my fortunes there. Should like to return & visit the Atlantic States once more & my old home, but there is a financial blockade established & I cannot run it.

Respects to Eliza & Frank. Remember me to Mr Boothe & all old friends

Yours Truly
Henry Eno

74. S. W. Knapp was a nephew of Henry's wife, Elizabeth.
75. The resources of Alpine County were so limited by 1869 that the California legislature passed a statute lowering the salaries of county officials. *The Alpine Miner,* March 13, 1869, reported: "The salary of County Judge is cut down from $1,800 to $1,000 a year and we learn it is the intention of the present worthy incumbent, Judge Eno. to leave the county within a few weeks."

Alpine County
Woodfords Nov 18 / 69

Wm Eno

       Dear Brother. This is Thanksgiving day & I thought I would write you. At this time of writing you are I presume about retiring for the night's rest & repose. It is 6 o'clock P M here. It is natural on this hallowed day to review the past. It saddens me. The record on a retrospect, shows badly, misspent time, opportunities neglected, and talents such as they are wasted. If my accounts were this day balanced I fear it would show against me. But if it should, & there is a future left me I must strive to get as much setoffs as possible, by untiring industry redeem past time, neglect no opportunity of doing good & exert my best abilities to prove that my life has not been altogether in vain. I have much to be thankful for. I have health & strength which few men of my age possess & I would not exchange them for wealth. I have still an unclouded intellect & a boyant & elastic spirit which misfortune has not subdued. So on the whole I think I have great reason to be thankful & perhaps I have great reason to be thankful that I am poor. These three words *I am poor* are more appalling to many than mene, mene, tekel, upharsin was to Beshasser [Belshassar] of old, but I am used to them & I well know the influence of good as well as bad habits. It dont trouble me as much as formerly

       I have bade good bye to Silver Mountain have been staying here a few days at the house [of] a friend. Shall leave next day after to morrow for Sacramento & from there expect to go to San Francisco take the Steamer for San Pedro, go to Los Angeles 28 miles in the interior & from there go on horseback over to the west side of the Sierra Nevada about

160 miles   I've not given up mining & never intend to.
Brother Ed writes me that Frank wants me to go into his
office while he attends to his Legislative duties, but I cant
reconcile it to myself to do so. I could earn a living I suppose but nothing more. I am unfitted for a City life & dont
believe I can stand civilization, so shall make one effort
more & if that fails make others. The section I go to is in a
very mild climate & the locality is on the west side of Death
Valley where rich mines have recently been discovered
inducements are offered me to go & I shall make the venture.
The name Death Valley dont deter me   I have in the
course of my pilgrimage on earth been several times very
near the dark valley of Death & "I still live". If I should
visit the Death Valley of California & "still live" I shall return to San Francisco & if able to return to Iowa & St Louis.
Have received a letter from John H Knapp of Wisconsin.[76]
He has gone to Europe with his son my namesake   he
goes for his health   he is now one of the richest men of
Wisconsin. I will write you from San Francisco. If you
write me direct to Sacramento care of E. H. Pomeroy Dep
Controller.[77] I dont know how long I may be detained
there, if absent, letters will be forwarded.

Yours truly

Henry Eno

I received a letter about a month ago from Miss Caroline
Eno of Erie Penn, inquiring if I was a relative. Her father
was from Hartford Conn. She writes that she knows no one
by the name of Eno, has no brother or sister & father &

76. John H. Knapp was the younger brother of Elizabeth Knapp Eno.
77. Erastus H. Pomeroy is listed as a clerk in the Controller's Office in
Sacramento in Robert E. Draper, *Sacramento City and County Directory
for 1869* (Sacramento, H. S. Crocker, 1869), p. 157. He resided at the
Waterhouse Building, corner of 8th and I streets.

mother both dead. Lives with her grandfather Simeon Dunn a man 88 years old.

Perhaps shall adopt your suggestion in a former letter & be a Correspondent for The Tribune. I've material enough for a volumn.

Death valley is said to be 400 feet below the level of the sea.

                                             Sacramento
Wm Eno   Nov 29 / 69
    Dear Brother
                 I arrived here day before yesterday. I bade good buy to Alpine County on the 24th & never expect to return to it. Stayed two days in Carson City took the railroad to Gold Hill a ride of a mile in an Omnibus took me to Virginia City from there took stage for Reno arrived there at ½ past eleven at night took the cars for Sacramento & next day at noon found myself safe sound & well at the Capitol of California. How long I shall be obliged to remain here cant say, but hope to leave within a week. I am trying to negotiate my Alpine County Warrants, have something over $1800. Will sell them for what I can get. Hope to obtain fifty cents on a dollar but it is somewhat doubtful. The money market is tight, tight, cant raise money on good security at three per cent per month. California the land of Gold & Nevada the land of Silver, have plenty of bullion & no money. May be compared to a man in the middle of water & perishing with thirst. I believe that the world over the richest mining Countries are the poorest, but I've cast my lot in them & must make the best of it. I hope to leave here for San Francisco within a week then take the Steamer for Los Angeles or rather San Pedro the port of entry & from

Los Angeles intend to go over the Sierra to Teheechaypah[78] near Walkers pass. Expect there to meet an old mountaineer to guide me to some mines recently discovered by a friend of mine. On his representations go to see & judge for myself   I am one of five locators of fifteen thousand feet of mining ground   if I find them as represented I can do well. Will write you from Los Angeles. I should like to have you write to that place

The Weather here is delightful. It is pleasant for me to see flowers in blossom in the gardens & door yards. I've seen no cultivated flowers before the past season. Over two months ago I saw ice at White Pine. When I left Alpine it was snowing & I faced the storm in an open carriage all day   here altho it is Nov & within one day of Winter it is spring. The grass is green & tomatoes & other semi-tropical vegitables are found in the gardens, radishes on the table every day. I hope & expect soon to be where no snow falls during the year, but had rather, far rather spend the winter where I could hear the Sleigh bells jingle & sit by a roaring fire the long winter nights. But "as we make our bed so must we lie" & I'll be contented & make the best of it. Respects to wife & Frank.

Yours Truly

Henry Eno

I asked you to next address me at Los Angeles, but think it best that you write to Sacramento, care of E. H. Pomeroy Dep

78. This is modern Tehachapi. The name was placed on the map as Tah-ee-chay-pah Pass by the Pacific Railroad Survey of 1853. The designation was obtained from local Indians. Fremont crossed the pass in 1844 and named a nearby creek Pass Creek. The name used by the Survey remained on the maps, with many variants of spelling, one of which was adopted by Eno. Edwin G. Gudde, *California Place Names: A Geographical Dictionary* (Berkeley, University of California Press, 1949), p. 355.

Controller. I am now stopping at his house. He is an old
acquaintance, a very good man considering he is a Democrat
& the brother of Brick Pomeroy[79] of execrable memory

                                        Los Angeles. Los Angeles Co
                                              Decr 26 1869

Wm Eno
Pine Plains
        Dear Brother
                Yours of the 12th Int was received yesterday & I
welcomed it as a Christmas gift. It was forwarded from
Sacramento by E. H. Pomeroy an old acquaintance of 18
years. He is a brother of *Brick* Pomeroy of infamous memory. He is a Democrat but a good Union Man. Having spent
five winters in the rugged climate of Alpine Co I thought I
would like to pass the sixth in a more genial clime. I was
here 18 years ago & find the place more improved in appearance than I am. The city limits are 6 miles square, with
a population of about 8000.[80] 18 Years has Americanized
the place very much. Then there were but few Americans
living here, the houses all built in the old Spanish style
with flat roofs. All the recent building has been in American
fashion. There are many foreigners living here, some French

79. *The Alpine Chronicle* of January 5, 1867, carried a front page
lead article entitled, "Punctuality: 'Brick' Pomeroy gets off the following
on 'Punctuality.'"

80. Bancroft reports that the city of Los Angeles was incorporated in
1850 and claimed a population of 2,500 in 1851, the year of Eno's first
visit. The United States census of 1870 recorded a population of 5,728
for the city and an additional 2,776 within the surrounding land survey
township, making a total of 8,504. Eno's estimate was surprisingly
accurate. *Ninth Census: Compendium of the Statistics of the Population
of the United States* (Washington, 1872), p. 91.

Italians but principally Germans & German Jews. There was then one small orange orchard about 12 years old had just commenced bearing & also a small orchard of English Walnut trees.[81] I visited it day before yesterday. The Orange trees are about 50 feet apart, as large as apple trees of like age & loaded with fruit. Should think there were several hundred bushels. Some ripe and all fast ripening. The English Walnut trees then small are now some 18 inches in diameter. The Walnuts sell redily here at 18 cent per lb. Each tree is worth from $25 to $30 per year. Oranges command $3 per hund. as high as $75 has been given for the fruit of one tree, but that was exceptional. At an auction the other day hundreds of orange lime & Citron trees were sold & some China tea shrubs. All the fruits growing in the Islands of the Meditteranian can be raised here. It is a semi tropical country. Roses & chrysanthemums are in full bloom. There is a good deal of excellent corn country & corn is now selling at 25 cents per bush. In fact everything ministering to the wants of men can here be raised, the climate is so genial & the soil so fruitful. But (there is a but to most every thing)

81. The first English walnuts were planted in Los Angeles County in 1857. They commenced bearing in three years, the crop increasing each year until the crop of 1863 amounted to 9,200 pounds. Previous to 1860 the walnuts used in California had been imported from China and Chile—nearly 30,000 pounds annually. The local product was soon considered better than the imported variety. Near San Gabriel Mission there were some exceptionally large walnut trees that had been set out by the missionaries. By 1870 there were over 15,000 walnut trees in Los Angeles County, one fourth of which were bearing well. The average yield was $30, and the crop was considered a sure one. One reporter noted: "The only trouble in gathering the fruit is the picking it up, as every nut disengages itself from its bark and falls to the ground full ripe." *Sacramento Daily Union*, November 15, 1862, February 5, 1870, December 16, 1871. Walnuts are also mentioned by H. D. Barrows, "Los Angeles Fifty Years Ago," *Annual Publication of the Historical Society of Southern California*, 6 (1905), 203–10.

men & women of energy & industry, they only flourish in
a northern clime. The people who have lived here for a
few years are intolerably lazy & indolent & Yankees who
come here & stay any length of time remind me of what
Goldsmith says in his Animated Nature (a book we had in
our Library I recollect) of the Wolf. He says "it has all the
bad qualities of the dog & none of his good ones"   so it
is with Yankees they imbibe all the bad qualities of the
Mexicans and none of their good ones. The fact is however
there are but few good ones to to be imbibed. The few days
I have been here is said to be very cold. Ice has been formed,
something unusual. Now the question arises Do the Inhabitants enjoy life here better than in Dutchess Co. I answer no. There is not so much thrift, full as much want.
They have no fire side comforts. There is not a public library
here. There is a congregational church, an Episcopalian &
a Catholic church. The Catholics are in the majority. I went
yesterday to the Episcopal Sunday school, some 25 scholars.
Returning past the Court house found there was a meeting of
the Methodists. The lower part of the Court house is a vault
for the Storage of brandies & liquors,[82] having a large
sign on the outside. As there was preaching above I was
reminded of an old stanza "There is a spirit above" "And
a spirit below" "The spirit of Love" "And the spirit of
woe" "The spirit above is the spirit divine" "The Spirit

82. The basement of the "Old Court House" in Los Angeles was
used as a wine cellar or depository by Kohler & Frohling for many years.
The upper story of this building, owned by John Temple, was converted
into a theater, where various dramatic companies, both English and
Spanish, played in the winter months. It often served as an auditorium
for public occasions such as the memorial services for Abraham Lincoln.
Apparently the Methodists used it for church services when it was not
otherwise engaged. H. D. Barrows, "Recollections of the Old Court
House and Its Builders," *Annual Publication of the Historical Society of
Southern California*, 3 (1894), 40–46.

below is the spirit of wine" so I went in & heard a very good sermon. The first time I imagine a liquor signboard ever induced a man to go to church

How long I shall remain here is uncertain   will depend upon advice I receive from Teheechaypah in Kern Co. I intend going over the Mountains to examine some silver Mines near Death Valley, reputed to be rich. I am one of the locators of 15000 feet. I did not go to White Pine soon enough, and I intend to have a White Pine of my own. But I may be dissappointed & if so, it wont be the first time, and I'll make the best of it. When I shall go is as I have said uncertain & it is uncertain when I return. Be governed by circumstances   When I go shall have the company of an old mountaineer   shall try & take good care of myself. Believe I shall be successful, but if not make the best of it. I hold that failures when they do not crush or dishearten a man lead to fortune & that obstacles to the resolute are only avenues to success. I wrote to Walter but have received no answer. I wish he would write me & say how my namesake Harry thrives. I'll write to Bell & Minnie & perhaps they will answer me. Best respects to Eliza. My love to all the young folks.

Yours Truly
Henry Eno

Los Angeles
Feby 10 1870

Wm Eno
    Dear Brother
        I leave this Angelic city next day after tomorrow to visit some mines on the West side of Death Valley. I go in company with a Mr Fuller who came down here expecting to find me. Go with him to Teheechaypah in

Kern Co from there expect to be accompanied by a Mr
Mellicain [?] to the mines about 120 miles from there.
Shall go that distance on hor[s]eback, carrying our blankets
& grub & camp out wherever night overtakes us & we
can get Water. its a dry country & long stretches between
springs of water, one of forty three miles. Fuller brought
down some 100 lbs of silver ore, as rich as any 100 lbs
I ever saw at White Pine.

From his representations & of others I believe it another
White Pine. Fuller & three others have 17 claims or lodes.
They offer me one fifth if I can find them a purchaser. The
ore he brought down will assay over $400 per ton. He says
there are five tons at one mine of equal richness. If he tells
me the truth the mines are worth an immense sum of
money, enough to satisfy even the dreams of avarice. I
want to have five tons of ore taken out & taken to San
Francisco & worked. If it works even $100 per ton it would
be a guarantee of a sale of the mines of at least $100,000.
To do this I have not the means on hand. I have money
enough to make the trip take me back to San Francisco &
something perhaps to spare. The transportation of the ore
will cost $80 or $90 per ton. Shall lack $300 to carry out
what I want to do   Am trying to make arrangements
here to raise the money giving a lien on the ore. Hope to
be successful, but whether I succeed or not am determined
to have 5 tons brought here & trust to the chapter of
accidents.

Next day after to morrow I expect to leave here & next
day after to morrow I shall be seventy two years old. I am
at that age as strong & vigorous as any one I know of equal
age. I cannot say as is said of Moses of old when 120 year
old, "That his eye was not dim neither was his strength
abated" but I can see well with Specs & I can look upon a

trip of 240 miles to Death Valley the greater part of the way on horseback without any fears but what I am equal to it. So I have abundant reason to be thankful to the giver of all good that though not blessed with wealth I am blessed with that which I prize more good health & furthermore I am blessed with a boyant elastic spirit which no reverses & misfortunes have crushed & I will work & strive while my day lasts. I am going beyond the region of post or Express offices but shall try to make arrangements to have letters forwarded by private hands. Have not received a letter from you since I have been here but have written once or twice. Hope to hear from you & that you will write on receiving this. Received a letter yesterday from brother Edward.

Los Angeles Co is suffering from drought. So is San Diego below here. Thousands of cattle are dying from starvation. A Mr. Foster[83] the owner of 25,000 head on a large ranch he owns in San Diego wrote to a friend of of his here that he kept six men employed all the time in skinning dead cattle & sheep. San Diego has a splendid harbor & a charming climate & nothing more. Los Angeles has fertile lands when water for irrigation can be found. Has a city of 7000 Inhabitants, has not a fire engine, no public library or reading room, no book store. It has charming orange groves & a lazy indolent dissolute licentious population, with some few exceptions & the exceptions as lawyers say "prove the truth of the rule". Nature has been lavish in her gifts, man has done but little. It is in truth the country described by the poet

"Where every prospect pleases
And only man is vile"

83. This is probably a reference to John Forster, a large ranch owner in Southern California, whose holdings were acquired during the Mexican period. Hubert Howe Bancroft, *History of California, 3,* 744. For

I expect to be absent some five or six weeks but shall be governed by circumstances. In all probability shall go to Cerro Gordo on Owens Lake[84] before I return to this place.

Was roused up about half past five in the morning by an alarm of fire. Found a large liquor establishment burning up or rather down. As I saw the smoke of the burning alcohol curling up I fancied the curses of widows & orphans on its makers & venders ascending with it to heaven & if a glass of water could have quenched the flames I would not have given it. Have written much more than I intended when I set down. Will close by wishing you & yours that health of body & peace of mind with out which wealth connot be enjoyed.

Very Truly Yours

Henry Eno

send you a Los Angeles paper containing a puff of the mines I expect to visit. It is a detestable copperhead secession firebrand of a newspaper.[85]

---

details concerning the ranch, see Terry E. Stephenson, "Forster vs. Pico," *Quarterly of the Historical Society of Southern California, 17* (December 1935), 143–47; *18* (March 1936), 22–30; (June 1936), 50–68.

84. The Cerro Gordo, or Lone Pine, District in the southern part of the Inyo Range, near Owens Lake, was organized in 1866. The year before Mexican miners had located the Ignacio, San Felipe, and San Francisco claims. Cerro Gordo City was 7,200 feet above sea level and nineteen miles by wagon road in a southeastern direction from the settlement at Lone Pine. This district was Inyo County's greatest producer of metal—an estimated $13,000,000. The activity there also encouraged mining exploration elsewhere. Raymond, *Statistics,* pp. 17–27. *Report of the California State Mineralogist, 1915–1916, 15* (Sacramento, 1919), 87–88. Chalfant, *Story of Inyo,* pp. 248–56. Chalfant, "Cerro Gordo," *Quarterly of the Historical Society of Southern California,* 22 (June 1940), 55–61.

85. This is probably a reference to the Los Angeles *Daily News,* possibly to the Los Angeles *Star.* A systematic search of the available files

Kern Co
Tehechaypah
Feby 20 / 70

Wm Eno

I arrived at this place day before yesterday, four days from Los Angeles. This point is the lowest pass on the Sierra Nevada & where the S.P.R.R. will probably run if constructed on the 35 parallel. The mines of El Paso[86] are distant from here some 60 miles. I expect to visit them & leave here in four or five days. Shall go on horseback or rather on Mule back. Go in company with a sober reliable youngish man a hardy mountaineer. From El Paso we expect to go to Lone Pine in Inyo Co & from there to the Panamett mines[87] on the west of Death Valley. Then intend to return to Los Angeles & from there to San Francisco. Have no fears but what I can stand the trip. [My health is good & camping out & leading a sort of vagabond wild life agrees with me]

Have not had a line from you the last two months. should like to have you on receipt of this write to me at Lone Pine Inyo Co Cal. [From everything I can hear & learn I am

---

of the newspapers in California has, however, failed to locate the article on either the El Paso Mines or the Panamint Range that Eno proposed to visit.

86. The El Paso Mountains were two groups of mountains north of Randsburg in Kern County. They were so named because of a nearby pass through which modern highway 395 now runs. Undoubtedly mining prospects had been located here. Gudde, *California Place Names*, p. 255.

87. The name Panamint was derived from a division of the Shoshonean Indians who formerly occupied the region. The range appears as Panamint in the report of the Nevada Boundary Commission in 1861 and was probably applied by the Darwin French party the preceding year. Gudde, p. 252.

induced to believe that the Panamett mines & El Paso are as
rich as can be found in the famous White Pine Country].

I wrote to Miss Bell some time ago. Would be pleased to
have a line from her to read on the Desert. Best respect to
all bearing the Eno name

Yours truly
Henry Eno

Lone Pine
Inyo Co
Cal
Wm Eno   March 22 1870
Dear Brother

I left Los Angeles on the 13th of Feb. Arrived
here a week ago. Leave to day in company with Geo Melican
& Aug. Ingram for the Panamett mines west of Death
Valley about 100 miles distant. From thence shall go to the
El Paso mines which I visited on my way up & from thence
to Los Angeles via Tehechaypah Kern County & from there
to San Francisco. My health is very good. Find I can stand
riding & camping out as well as ever. Sort of like this vagabond life, but hope some day to settle down with enough to
live on where I can hold communion with those to whom
I am connected by kindred ties.

Remember me kindly to Eliza Stewart Frank & Walter
& all my grand nephews & nieces. I shall probably be in Los
Angeles in four or five weeks. Should like receive a line
from you. Have recd no letters from Pine Plains the last
three months

Yours truly
Henry Eno

                                                     Kern Co
                                                  Tehechaypay
Wm Eno   April 21 1870
     Dear Brother
          Arrived here yesterday safe sound & in excellent
health. Wrote you several times from several out of the
way places. Have not heard from you the last three months.
Stood the trip to Death Valley & so far back better than I
expected. Am in just the right trim for another campain but
must return (much to my regret) to the civilized portion of
Gods earth   have faith to believe that I shall not lose
my journey. Have found mines rich as any even in White
Pine hope to profit by them & could to a great amount where
[were] I differently circumstanced. Write me to San Francisco. Am obliged to write briefly.
                              Yours truly
                                        Henry Eno

Love to wife & family

E. D. Sawyer
M. H. Myrick[88]

                     LAW OFFICE OF SAWYER & MYRICK,
                              No 621 Clay Street,
                         San Francisco, Aug 15th 1870

Wm Eno Esq
     Dear Sir.
          On yesterday I called by request on your brother
Hon. Henry Eno. He has been unwell for several weeks &
has wholly or nearly exhausted his means and is owing some

----

88. Milton Hills Myrick was a law partner of E. D. Sawyer between
1869 and 1871. Myrick had come to California in 1854 by the Nicaragua
route. For a time he worked as a printer on the San Francisco *Sun* and in
1855 assisted in establishing the Shasta *Republican*. He was trained in

bills for board, washing &c. He is about his room but quite
feeble. He must have pecuniary assistance and he requested
me to address you & his bro. at St. Louis for assistance. I have
just finished a letter Mr Edward I. Eno—St. L. Your brother
needs about $200 in gold to pay his bills and take him to
St Louis where he hopes to proceed to Iowa as his health &
means will permit. He asks you to send his letters to my
care, any draft to his order.

I think he should leave here by the 15th of Sept. Whatever you do in the matter please do at once. Permit me to
suggest that you send, if you can, a draft for the sum and
inform your brother at St L—of your action or if you cannot
do so request him to do it. After what I have written I need
not state that he *must have pecuniary assistance,* and this
should come as I have no doubt it will, from his brothers
rather than strangers.

Your obt servt

E D Sawyer

San Francisco

Sept 12 1870

Dear Brother

It is now nearly three months since I have written
to you & for most of that time have been unable to. Soon

---

law in Red Bluff. He moved to San Francisco in 1866. His partnership
with Sawyer terminated in 1871 when he was elected probate judge of
the city and county of San Francisco. After a four-year term, he was
renominated by the Republicans and elected. Between 1880 and 1887
he served as associate justice of the Supreme Court of California. Shuck,
History, pp. 726–30. See also *San Francisco: Her Great Manufacturing,
Commercial, and Financial Institutions, 1904–1905* (San Francisco,
Pacific Art Co., 1904–05), pp. 84, 85; *The Alta California Commercial
Edition, 1889,* San Francisco Pamphlets, 7, No. 7, 22, in the California
State Library, Sacramento.

after my return from Los Angeles I was taken sick, had a dysentery, which almost prostrated me. As a last resort a Doctor gave me Ladanum [laudanum] which I never could take without making me half crazy. It was a long time before I could get over the effects of it. I am now very nervous, but am getting strong every day. When able to walk about I weighed only 142 lbs. Believe I shall soon regain my usual health & strength. Judge E D Sawyer & other friends called to see me often. When enfeebled by my complaint, I reccollect asking Judge to write you—I certainly should not have done so had I been well. He tells me he wrote that I wished to go to St Louis but had no means. Since my return I have been peculiarly unfortunate   had a pocket book containing mining stock worth $150 & two County Warrants one of $110 & the other of $150 Stolen. The mining stock & County Warrants were endorsed by me having once pledged & redeemed them. I can get no trace of them & am afraid it is a dead loss. I have got the police in search. The expenses consequent on sickness absorbed all my money & left me poor indeed. I only wonder I have kept up at all. The darkest time it is said is just before day, so I still have hope. I believe I shall still make my tour to the South pay. Dont give up. However I confess that I have been nearer discouraged than I ever was before. There is nothing that brings down the pride of manhood more than sickness. It is bad enough of itself, but to be sick, to have none but strangers to lend a helping hand, to sooth & sympathise with you is bad indeed. But it is not comforting to look back & reflect that it is ones own fault. But I'll make the best I can of it. I'll write again in a few days.

Yours truly

Henry Eno

E. D. Sawyer,
M. H. Myrick.

LAW OFFICE OF SAWYER & MYRICK,
No. 621 Clay Street,
San Francisco, Feby 3 1871

Wm Eno

Dear Brother

The Prodigal son leaves this morning on twenty
four hours preparation for New York on the Steamship
Colorado via the Isthmus. My health would not permit the
overland route   to stay here was to die, it cant be worse
to go. If I arrive at New York will call on your Son in Law
Ellis. I hope not to be an incumbrance on any one. Shall
earnestly try to help myself   how God only knows.

Yours truly

Henry Eno

BIBLIOGRAPHY

Manuscripts and Pamphlets

CALIFORNIA:

The Bancroft Library, University of California:
Papers of the Imperial Silver Quarries Company, Ltd., Companies Registration Office, Program for the Collection of Western Americana in Great Britain.
California State Library, Sacramento:
California Pioneer Biographical Sketches, Card File.
Hunt, Rockwell D., "The Prince of California Pioneers." Typewritten manuscript of address delivered at Bidwell Centenary, Chico, May 19, 1941.
Records of the Families of California Pioneers, Daughters of the American Revolution of California. Typescript.
Romantic Forty-niners, Daughters of the American Revolution Pioneer Records, 1950.
Royce, Charles C., *In Memorium John Bidwell*. Three-volume scrapbook on life and accomplishments of Bidwell.
Some Facts About Gold and Silver Mines and Mining, also the Prospectus of the Globe Gold and Silver Mining Company, New York, J. Winchester, 1872.
The Alta California Commercial Edition, 1889. Copy bound in San Francisco Pamphlets, 7, No. 7.

CONNECTICUT:

Western Americana Collection, Yale University Library, New Haven:
Edward Eno Papers. Nineteen letters and other papers be-

tween various members of the Eno family, chiefly those written by Edward to his brother William, 1839–57.

Henry Eno Papers. Forty-five letters, chiefly those of Henry Eno to his brother William, 1849–71.

ILLINOIS:

Chicago Historical Society:
Eno Manuscripts. Sixteen letters and other papers written by or addressed to members of the Eno family, chiefly those of Edward, 1854–57.

IOWA:

Iowa State Department of History and Archives, Des Moines:
Vital Statistics of Lee County pioneers, compiled by the Daughters of the American Revolution.

State University of Iowa Library, Iowa City:
Eno Letters. Fifty-one letters, chiefly those of Henry Eno to his father Stephen and some to his brother William, 1813–57.

The State Historical Society of Iowa Library, Iowa City:
Census of Iowa Territory, 1840, Lee County, Fort Madison.

NEW YORK:

The New York State Library, Albany:
Stephen Eno Papers. Eno family letters and documents, 1745–1908, in two boxes. Materials primarily concerned with Stephen Eno, his son William Eno, and William's two sons, William Stewart Eno and Frank Eno. Fourteen scrapbooks of selected newspaper clippings of the Civil War years prepared by Frank Eno are also available.

Newspapers

CALIFORNIA:

The Alpine Chronicle (Markleeville and Silver Mountain), scattered issues, 1866–1869, Bancroft Library.

Calaveras *Chronicle* (Mokelumne Hill), scattered issues, 1851–1853, Bancroft Library.

Daily Evening Bulletin (San Francisco), May 14, 1856, California State Library.

Monitor Gazette, scattered issues, 1864–1866. Continued as *The Alpine Miner,* scattered issues, 1866–1869, Bancroft Library.

Sacramento Bee, January 28, 1896.

Sacramento Daily Record-Union, March 7, 1887.

Sacramento Daily Union, scattered issues, 1853–1868, California State Library.

San Francisco *Call,* March 26, 1909.

San Francisco *Daily Alta California,* scattered issues, 1850–1865, California State Library.

San Francisco Daily Whig, August 11, 1853, California State Library.

Silver Mountain Bulletin, scattered issues, 1866–1867, Bancroft Library.

Yreka Journal, March 24 and 31, 1909.

IOWA:

The Fort Madison Patriot, 1, May 2, 1838.

Iowa News (Dubuque), *1,* November 24, 1837 and May 26, 1838, State Historical Society of Iowa, Iowa City.

NEVADA:

White Pine News, June 15 and October 10, 1869, Bancroft Library.

Government Documents

Browne, J. Ross, *Letter to the Secretary of the Treasury, Transmitting Report upon the Mineral Resources of the States and Territories West of the Rocky Mountains,* Washington, 1867.
———, *Report on the Mineral Resources of the States and Territories West of the Rocky Mountains,* Washington, 1868.

Browne, J. Ross and James W. Taylor, *Reports upon the Mineral Resources of the United States, 1867,* Washington, 1867.

"California Message and Correspondence," House Executive Document 17, 31 Cong., 1 sess., 1849–1850, 528–36. Report of Richard B. Mason on discovery of gold in California.

Eno, Edward I., *Second Annual Report of the Illinois State Sanitary Commission . . . January 1, 1864 to January 1, 1865,* 81–83, Springfield, 1865.

"Fort Barrancas Military Reservation," Senate Executive Document 103, 41 Cong., 2 sess., 1869–1870.

Hague, James D., *Mining Industry,* Vol. 3 in Clarence King *The United States Geological Exploration of the Fortieth Parallel,* Professional Papers of the Engineer Department, U. S. Army, No. 18, Washington, 1870.

Laws of the Territory of Iowa, 1838–1839, 1840–1841, 1842–1843.

Maule, William M., *A Contribution to the Geographical and Economic History of the Carson, Walker, and Mono Basins,* San Francisco, Forest Service, U. S. Department of Agriculture, 1938.

Raymond, Rossiter W., *Statistics of Mines and Mining in the States and Territories West of the Rocky Mountains, 1870,* House Executive Document 10, 42 Cong., 1 sess., 1871, Washington, 1872, 17–27, 51–53.

Report of the California State Mineralogist, 1915–1916, 15, Sacramento, 1919.

Shambaugh, B. F., ed., *Executive Journal of Iowa, 1838–1841.*

Articles

Barrows, H. D., "Los Angeles Fifty Years Ago," *Annual Publication of the Historical Society of Southern California,* 6 (1905), 203–10.

————, "Recollections of the Old Court House and Its Builders," *Annual Publication of the Historical Society of Southern California,* 3 (1894), 40–46.

Chalfant, W. A., "Cerro Gordo," *Quarterly of the Historical Society of Southern California,* 22 (June 1940), 55–61.

Clark, Dan Elbert, "The Beginnings of Liquor Legislation in Iowa," *Iowa Journal of History and Politics,* 5 (1907), 193–212.

Curti, Merle E., "Young America," *American Historical Review,* 32 (1926), 34–55.

"The Early Bar of Lee County," *Annals of Iowa,* 1st ser. 9 (July 1871), 613–16.

Elliott, Russell Richard, "The Early History of White Pine County, Nevada, 1865–1871," *Pacific Northwest Quarterly,* 30 (April 1939), 145–68.

"H. G. Blasdel, Nevada's First Governor, 1865–1870," *Nevada Highways and Parks,* 22 (November 1, 1962), 18–19.

Historical Bulletin of the Calaveras County Historical Society, 1, April 1953.

Las Calaveras, Quarterly Bulletin of the Calaveras County Historical Society, 4, January 1956.

Pelzer, Louis, "The History and Principles of the Democratic Party in the Territory of Iowa," *Iowa Journal of History and Politics,* 6 (1908), 3–54.

Stephenson, Terry E., "Forster vs. Pico," *Quarterly of the Historical Society of Southern California,* 17 (December 1935), 143–47; 18 (March 1936), 22–30; (June 1936), 50–68.

Taylor, Hawkins, "Before and after the Territorial Organization of Iowa," *Annals of Iowa,* 1st ser. 9 (January 1871), 450–57.

———, "Early Men and Early Days Recalled," *Annals of Iowa,* 1st ser. 10 (January 1872), 25–31.

———, "Law Ministers of the Olden Time," *Annals of Iowa,* 1st ser. 9 (July 1871), 606–13.

"Territorial Convention of 1837," *Iowa Journal of History and Politics,* 9 (1911), 385–407.

Van der Zee, Jacob, "The Opening of the Des Moines Valley," *Iowa Journal of History and Politics,* 14 (1916), 479–558.

"The Writing of Judge George G. Wright," *Annals of Iowa,* 3rd ser. 11 (January 1915), 594–99.

Periodicals

Gleason's Pictorial Drawing Room Companion, 5, December 24, 1853.
Hutchings' Illustrated California Magazine, 3, San Francisco, Hutchings & Rosenfield, May 1859.
Mining and Scientific Press, 1–23, 1860–71.
San Francisco News Letter, 30, April 24, 1880.

Encyclopedias and Reference Works

The Americana . . . Biographies, New York, Americana Corp., 1929.
Culver, J. Horace, *The Sacramento City Directory*, Sacramento City, Transcript Press, 1851.
Draper, Robert E., *Sacramento City and County Directory for 1869*, Sacramento, H. S. Crocker, 1869.
Historical Encyclopedia of Illinois, Chicago, 1901.
Mitzakis, Marcel, *The Oil Encyclopedia*, New York, John Wiley, 1922.
Morgan, Dale, *California Manuscripts: Being a Collection of Important, Unpublished & Unknown Original Historical Sources*, New York, Edward Eberstadt, 1961.
National Cyclopaedia of American Biography, 11.
Ninth Census: Compendium of the Statistics of the Population of the United States, Washington, 1872.

Books

Ayers, James J., *Gold and Sunshine: Reminiscences of Early California*, Boston, Gorham Press, 1922.
Bailey, Thomas A., *A Diplomatic History of the American People*, New York, Appleton-Century-Crofts, 1958.
Bancroft, Hubert Howe, *Chronicles of the Builders of the Commonwealth*, 7, San Francisco, History Co., 1892.
——, *History of California*, 3, 6, 7 (*Works*, 20, 23, 24), San Francisco, History Co., 1888–90.

Bemis, Samuel F., *The American Secretaries of State and Their Diplomacy*, 6, New York, Alfred A. Knopf, 1928.

———, *A Short History of American Foreign Policy and Diplomacy*, New York, Henry Holt, 1959.

Borthwick, J. D., *Three Years in California*, Edinburgh and London, William Blackwood, 1857.

Browne, J. Ross, *Resources of the Pacific Slope*, New York, D. Appleton, 1869.

Camp, Charles L., *John Doble's Journal and Letters from the Mines, 1851–1865*, Denver, Old West Publishing Co., 1963.

Caughey, John W., *Gold Is the Cornerstone*, Berkeley, University of California Press, 1949.

Chalfant, W. A., *The Story of Inyo*, published by the author, 1922.

Davis, Winfield J., *History of Political Conventions in California, 1849–1892*, Sacramento, Publications of the California State Library, 1893.

Evans, Albert S., *White Pine: Its Geographical Location, Topography, Geological Formation; Mining Laws; Mineral Resources; Towns; Surroundings; Climate; Population, Altitude, and General Characteristics; Conditions of Society; How to Reach There; What It Costs to Get There and Life There; When to Go There, etc., etc.* San Francisco, Alta California Printing House, 1869.

Gidden, Paul Henry, *The Birth of the Oil Industry*, New York, MacMillan, 1938.

———, *Pennsylvania Petroleum, 1750–1872. A Documentary History*, Titusville, Pennsylvania Historical Museum Commission, 1947.

Gudde, Erwin G., *California Place Names: A Geographical Dictionary*, Berkeley, University of California Press, 1949.

Guinn, J. M., *History of the State of California and Biographical Record of the San Joaquin Valley, California*, Chicago, Chapman Publishing Co., 1905.

Harris, Henry, *California's Medical Story*, Springfield, Ill., Charles C. Thomas, [Printed by Grabhorn Press], 1932.

History of Lee County, Iowa, Chicago, Western Historical Co., 1879.

Hittell, John S., *A History of the City of San Francisco and Incidentally of the State of California,* San Francisco, A. L. Bancroft, 1878.

Hittell, Theodore H., *History of California, 3, 4,* San Francisco, N. J. Stone, 1897.

Huntting, Isaac, *History of Little Nine Partners of North East Precinct, and Pine Plains, New York, Duchess County,* Amenia, N.Y., Chas. Walsh, 1897.

Jackson, W. Turrentine, *Treasure Hill: Portrait of a Silver Mining Camp,* Tucson, University of Arizona Press, 1963.

Jones, Joseph Roy, *Memories, Men and Medicine: A History of Medicine in Sacramento, California with Biographies of the Founders,* Sacramento Society for Medical Improvement, 1950.

A Memorial and Biographical History of the Counties of Merced, Stanislaus, Calaveras, Tuolumne and Mariposa, California, Chicago, Lewis Publishing Co., 1892.

Nadeau, Remi A., *City Makers,* Garden City, N.Y., Doubleday, 1948.

Paul, Rodman W., *California Gold,* Cambridge, Harvard University Press, 1947.

Peck, Anne Merriman, *The March of Arizona History,* Tucson, Arizona Silouettes, 1962.

Phelps, Alonzo, *Contemporary Biography of California's Representative Men,* San Francisco, A. L. Bancroft, 1882.

Power, Robert H., *Pioneer Skiing in California,* Vacaville, Calif., Nut Tree, 1960.

Rock, Francis John, *J. Ross Browne: A Biography,* Washington, Catholic University of America, 1929.

San Francisco: Her Great Manufacturing, Commercial and Financial Institutions, 1904-1905, San Francisco, Pacific Art Co., 1904-05.

Shuck, Oscar T., *History of the Bench and Bar of California,* Los Angeles, Commercial Printing House, 1901.

Smith, James H., *History of Duchess County, New York: Illustrations and Biographical Sketches, Some of Its Prominent Men and Pioneers*, Syracuse, N.Y., D. Mason, 1882.

Stewart, Watt, *Henry Meiggs, Yankee Pizarro*, Durham, Duke University Press, 1946.

Stiles, Edward H., *Recollections and Sketches of Notable Lawyers and Public Men in Early Iowa*, Des Moines, Homestead Publishing Co., 1916.

The Bay of San Francisco: The Metropolis of the Pacific Coast and Its Suburban Cities, 2, Chicago, Lewis Publishing Co., 1892.

Wood, Richard Coke, *Calaveras, the Land of Skulls*, Sonora, Calif., Mother Lode Press, 1955.

INDEX

52–56, 110–12; residence destroyed by fire in *1854,* 56; move to Campo Seco, 56–57, 115; birth of daughter, 57; father's estate, 57, 116–17; effect of panic of *1854–55,* 59–60, 122–23; Amador Canal Co., 59, 129; San Francisco Vigilante Committee of *1856,* 61, 124–25; candidate for judge of Calaveras County, 61–63, 65, 127–28; moves to Alpine County, 66–67, 131; presides over meeting of Union men, 68; judge of Alpine County, 69–71, 137–39; conflict with owner of *Alpine Chronicle,* 70–71, 137–38; views as judge, 71–74; role as lecturer and author, 74–78, 166; decision re lumbering operations, 78–79; conflict with Alpine County over salary, 79–81, 166; political involvement in *1867* election, 81–85; indictment by grand jury and reply, 85–89; visits Treasure Hill, Nev., 92–94, 179–90; decision not to run for re-election, 94, 191; mining activities in southern California, 95–96, 173–74, 193–205; departure for the East, 97, 208; last days, 97–98; comments on Spanish land grants, 104; on presidential election, 125–28; on Pacific Railroad, 112, 127; on life in Alpine County, 134–35, 139–40, 142–46, 151–54, 166–67; considers running for District Judge, 147; interested in purchasing real estate, 147–48; reports on winter sports in Alpine County, 153, 153 n.; mining developments in Alpine County, 161–63; concerning judgeship, 162–64; reflections on his career, 192; plans to go to southern California, 192–93; descrip-

tion of Los Angeles, 196–99, 201–02
Eno, Mary, daughter of William Eno, 108, 108 n., 110, 126–27
Eno, Mary Denton, wife of Stephen Eno, 3
Eno, Rose: family role, 26 n., 114 n., 124; Henry Eno's concern for, 114, 118
Eno, Rufus: birth, 6; concern of Henry Eno, 11–12, 25–26; leaves family home, 25; death, 26, 26 n.
Eno, Stephen: early life, 1–6; death, 57, 113; Henry Eno's comments on his life, 113; public tribute, 113–14 n.; settlement of estate, 116–17, 119
Eno, Stewart, son of William Eno, 11, 108, 108 n., 123
Eno, Walter, son of William Eno, 97, 108, 131, 186, 199
Eno, William: birth, 3; education, 4; success in youth, 8; advances money to Edward, 27, 32; Henry requests financial assistance, 38–39, 60, 104, 129; administers father's estate, 57, 116–17; learns of Henry's plans to return, 97; urged by Henry to come to California, 127, 139
Evans, Albert S., 93

Farming in Illinois, 32
Fire: at Mokelumne Hill, *1854,* 56, 114 n.; at Campo Seco, *1859,* 65
Folger, R. M.: as proprietor of *Alpine Chronicle,* 66; political activities, 69–70, 81–85; split with Eno, 70–71, 86–89; biographical sketch, 131–32 n.
Forster, John, 201, 201–02 n.
Fort Barrancas, Fla., 133–34 n.
Fort Madison, Iowa, 14, 16, 30, 35
"French War," conflict between miners at Mokelumne Hill, 45